# A DIFFERENT DRUM

*Constance Carpenter Cameron*

*PRENTICE-HALL, INC., Englewood Cliffs, New Jersey*

**Library of Congress Cataloging in Publication Data**

Cameron, Constance Carpenter.
  A different drum.

    1.  Aphasia—Personal narratives.  I.  Title.
RC425.C35    362.7'8'24  [B]    73–7801
ISBN 0–13–211524–7

*To the memory of*
MARION LEWIS PITKIN
*Who had resolved to make hers a*
*meaningful voice in the world of aphasia*
*Just before it was stilled*

# Acknowledgments

Thomas W. Ward, Jr., Ph.D., for his introduction.

Mrs. Joanne Ratcliff, M.S. in Journalism, U.C.L.A., for her editing services.

*The Brain-injured Child in Home, School and Community,* Dr. William M. Cruickshank, Syracuse University Press, 1967.

*Success Through Play,* D. H. Radler with Dr. Newell C. Kephart, Harper & Row, 1960.

*A Teaching Method for Brain-injured and Hyperactive Children,* Dr. William M. Cruickshank, Frances A. Bentzen, Frederick H. Ratzeburg, Miriam T. Tannhauser, Syracuse University Press, 1961.

# Introduction

My original impressions of Evan were summarized as:

*Functioning retarded, subsequent to or in addition to neurological impairment; including both expressive and receptive aphasia; intellectual potential unknown.*

My written description of him began, "Evan is a blond-haired, handsome three-year-old . . ."

I remember he made no objection to accompanying me but did look back toward his parents as we walked down the hall. My report stated, "No real rapport was ever established except that he would smile with the examiner occasionally." At this time he walked poorly and only spoke a few words.

As a rule he did not respond to toys or test objects except to smell or taste them. He seemed to enjoy putting toys away or throwing them on the floor. He did run a car back and forth on the table top, but this appeared to be more movement than actual playing. Several times he left his chair to run back and forth, stopping himself at the walls with his hands; or he would wander aimlessly about the room; or he would sit doing nothing. Attention span deficiencies were severe.

This was Evan at three years of age: Prognosis, very guarded.

Many children are born into this world with certain isolating limitations that cause them to go through life unlearned, unresponsive and unhappy. And so they remain unless some teacher takes the time and effort to build a bridge between the child and the world. Helen

Keller was such a child; Evan Cameron, about whom this story is written, is such a child.

This saga is unfinished and perhaps never will be finished, but the heroic efforts and unexpected successes already wrought are important to the people of a world that needs courage and faith. I say unexpected successes —unexpected and doubted by most people who evaluate and treat children with Evan's problems. But certainly not unexpected by his mother and father, who believed and then backed their faith with works.

There was no cookbook available to guide the Camerons when they undertook the job which was theirs. True, there were isolated cases of success with children of this type before, but no one had attempted to directly compile a list of the concepts that are unknown to a child with aphasia and must be taught! Furthermore, there is very little information on the methods of teaching such concepts. For each child this is a new area that requires inventiveness and perseverance. First a bridge must be forged between child and one person, then generalized out to the rest of the world.

The number of times that these parents' fatigue, doubt and anger threatened to interrupt or halt Evan's progress is not emphasized. Failure was the rule, however, and success the exception.

What more Evan must endure, how far Evan can go and what emotional scars Evan will carry are still unknown, but love of the child and the undying faith seem to be winning. Evan is making it.

Thomas W. Ward, Jr., Ph.D.
Clinical Psychologist
Children's Hospital of Orange County, California

A *phasic.* Our little boy could not understand speech. The bright, intelligent child so easily glimpsed through the blue eyes was locked away from us: unreachable, unable to reach us. As I numbly prepared Evan for his nap, the psychologist's words echoed and reechoed in my mind.

"His aphasia is of such a severe nature . . . can't even ascertain if he has a normal potential inside or not . . . even if he does, the chances of getting to it. . . ."

How could fate be so malicious? It seemed that with deliberately planned cruelty we had been enticed into an illusion that we had been rarely blessed, only so that we could be hurt the more. Kissing Evan's rosy cheek, I hugged him tightly, but without the joy that had been mine since an evening just over three years before.

"Here he comes—yes—it's the boy!" The doctor lifted the infuriated little creature close to my face. "See? There's no doubt about that!"

I watched, almost unbelieving, as the doctor laid the baby on my stomach. With a swift gesture, he cleared the tiny throat, making way for the first angry yells. A boy! I knew nothing about little boys! What kind of mother would I be to one? My husband and I had been certain that we would have another little girl. We already had two small daughters, seven-year-old Cynthia (Cindy) and six-year-old Wendy, and, by coincidence, most of our closest friends had only girls. It seemed unlikely that we would be the ones to break the pattern. Secretly, I wasn't sure that I wanted to. I had hoped that both Cindy and Wendy would be girls, and Don and I had taken great pleasure in them. My doctor, on the other hand, had been just as certain as we were not that this would be a boy. Not because of a distinctive heartbeat nor any of the usual reasons but because we already *had* two girls,

1

and it was time for our boy. Although an obstetrician, Dr. Ryan was obviously one of those physicians who had never gotten over the thrill of bringing a child into the world. Now his jubilance over my son seemed to me to lend exceptional importance to the event.

At length, absorbing the fact that I indeed had a little boy, I began to examine every aspect of him. He was still very literally a part of me as he lay on my stomach, the umbilical cord still intact. Arms, legs, everything was there and well formed, and—oh! I thought—what a beautiful head! The tiny facial features were comically familiar, and I giggled, "He looks just like my husband."

As part of a national campaign, our television set had been constantly proclaiming the last several weeks "Birth Defect Month," and this had kept me uncomfortably mindful of the uncertainties of birth. "You know," I had remarked to my husband after one of these messages, "I simply could not go through a tragedy involving one of my children. Death, or some terrible defect—I just couldn't take it."

"Well, you know, you'd have to, honey," Don had replied.

I now sought to put all worries on this score to rest. "His skin," I said anxiously to a nurse, "isn't it a funny color?"

"No, dear, it's fine. It's just these lights," she assured me.

Accepting this and finally content that my baby was healthy and whole, I relaxed and abandoned myself to the new feeling. I, the mother of a son! It seemed almost as strange a sensation as becoming a mother for the first time.

"What's his name?" asked the nurse who was taking down the vital statistics.

"Evan." I pronounced the name proudly.

"That's Celtic!" an Irish nurse remarked admiringly.

2

"Yes," I agreed, happily. "It means 'young warrior.'"

The little boy with the brave name was weighed—six pounds, fourteen ounces—measured, hand- and foot-printed, equipped with an identification bracelet and, at length, taken off to the mysterious recesses of the hospital. Dr. Ryan and a nurse bundled me into a hospital bed and wheeled me into the corridor where Don waited, a slightly dazed expression on his face.

Now that the excitement was over, I was slipping into the euphoria produced by the drug I had been given during labor and I was only dimly aware of the conversation between Don and the doctor as, together, they wheeled me to my room. Something about boys . . .

Even before I opened my eyes the next morning, my mind was wholly occupied by Evan Cameron. I wondered where the nursery was and if he was sleeping or awake and crying. I thought of him as he had looked the night before, lying on my stomach, kicking and screaming with rage at being pushed out of his warm, comfortable nest, and I wanted to hold him and make him feel safe again. Did Cindy and Wendy know yet that they had a little brother? They had been so excited yesterday but, like Don and me, not quite able to absorb the fact that the day we had awaited for so many months was actually upon us.

It had begun as all other days had recently. I had gone about my household routine, like many women in the final weeks of pregnancy, dull with the sensation of being in a limbo of waiting. Don, a high school history teacher, had come home early in the afternoon to drive me to the doctor's office for my weekly checkup. My pregnancy had been extremely uncomfortable, and during the last four months walking had become progressively more difficult. The movements of the baby's head were painful, becoming more severe in the afternoon and evening, forcing me off my feet. I sometimes wondered how I would recognize labor when it came. Indeed, as early as three months before, I had called the doctor in such pain that I was sure premature labor had begun. Since that one incident, the doctor had seemed to find no cause for worry, and in truth I had said little about my chronic troubles. I accepted my discomfort as being the result of weakened muscles. A friend who claimed to have had the same trouble with her third pregnancy said that that was the explanation her obstetrician gave and he was also unconcerned about it. So, not wanting to sound like a whining complainer over perfectly normal symptoms, I had put on a cheerful front during my prenatal examinations. This day, however, when the doctor had asked me how I felt, I blurted out, "I'm absolutely miserable!"

Dr. Ryan eyed me sympathetically. "Well," he said thoughtfully, "would you like to have it tonight? The baby's ready if you are."

"Would I!" I exclaimed. I realized he was talking about inducing the labor and had not anticipated that I would be a candidate for this. With instructions from Dr. Ryan to be at the hospital at six o'clock that evening, I returned to the waiting room and informed my husband of the turn of events. Don, who always played his new-father role in a gratifyingly typical manner, immediately became a bundle of nerves.

At home I put a few extra things into my already half-packed suitcase and shampooed the girls' hair. I had just done my own hair and, as it was Friday, the house was freshly cleaned, so I felt that all was in order. The only thing left to do was to drive to the hospital.

My labor was very short, two or three hours. The first birth-inducing injection had resulted in irregular, small contractions, but the second shot brought me very swiftly to delivery.

Such an organized way to have a baby, I thought now,

4

as I enjoyed the luxury of lying in bed in the morning. I felt really ready to enjoy my stay in the hospital, knowing that all the details for Don's and the children's comfort had been taken care of and the house was ready to bring the baby home to. I was pleased with myself, my baby, my family—pleased with the world.

Later that day when I held my baby for the first time, my contentment became almost achingly intense. I noted again his perfectly shaped head, the tiny ears nestled flat against it. His features were exquisite in their perfection, framed by soft golden hair. If, however, his beauty seemed somewhat unearthly, his temper certainly did not. He let me know from the outset that he preferred to be held in a vertical position rather than cradled horizontally and, when I tried the latter position, he expressed his displeasure with angry yells.

"He's full of hell!" I told my doctor later, and we beamed delightedly at each other.

The girls, too, had been particularly beautiful babies at birth. Cindy had looked like one of the early Dydee dolls (when the manufacturers had made them the way people wanted babies to look rather than the way they more often did). Plump and rosy-cheeked, she had soft dark hair and big violet-blue eyes that promised to turn to brown. Wendy, at barely more than five pounds, had appeared almost breathtakingly fragile. Yet, like Cindy's, the delicate pink and white skin was smooth and unwrinkled, and the finely molded features were set off by the same golden hair that now crowned this little boy.

I had hardly dared hope that this bonus of beauty would occur for a third time. Lord knew, it was enough just to have a healthy baby and, although relatively unconcerned about this primary consideration during my first two youthful pregnancies, I had sent up several prayers about it this time. To have all of my babies com-

5

pletely normal and, in addition, each touched with a unique beauty, made me feel in some way singled out. Perhaps everyone is given perfection in some one aspect of his life, I reflected. If so, then this was mine—beautiful, perfect babies. A special gift planned for me.

We enjoyed the infancy of our "tag-along" child in that relaxed fashion conferred upon experienced parents. We were unencumbered by the worries and self-doubts of new parenthood and, more than that, we were not impatient to rush time. Experience had taught us that Evan would sit, creep and walk soon enough, and we were content to savor each delightful baby stage without trying to hurry the next along. I sometimes looked at the girls and wondered, like Emily in *Our Town*, how I had let time slip by without fully *realizing* each moment. With this sometimes almost aching awareness of the impermanence of things, I hugged to me this later infancy —this perhaps last chance.

Our pleasure in Evan was even more complete because our daughters were of an age to really share it with us. At six and seven their maternal instincts had already been awakened by the weighty responsibilities involved in caring for a large family of dolls. Now they were delighted with having a real baby. Always a rather close little family, the four of us formed an affectionate, attentive circle around this newest member, and never did an infant have more devoted admirers. Since we had brought him home from the hospital, Evan had slept through the night without waking for a feeding. Also from the start, he had let us know that he would sleep in the cradle, but we could forget about the crib—the moment we lowered him into this larger bed he set up a series of howls that could not be ignored. Thinking that surely he could not tell that much difference between the two beds—except for the size, the mattresses and sheets were just alike—we attempted again and again to settle him into the disdained crib. He only became the more discerning, however, and his lusty protests would begin even before he was fully lowered onto the sheet. No one else had a baby so beautiful, so good, so intelligent, we assured each other. And realizing that our pride bordered on the obnoxious, we had to work hard not to gloat in the presence of others.

Evan seemed to sense his importance from the beginning and, being one of those babies who does not sleep a great deal, he loudly demanded our company when awake. Only too eager to oblige, Don and I took turns holding him, the girls rocked his cradle, or we just propped him in his infant seat in our midst. So long as he was with us, he was content.

"Who would believe a two-week-old baby could already be spoiled!" exclaimed my mother-in-law, who, on a visit, found herself a not unwilling slave of the tiny extrovert. More than happy to hold him during ninety-eight percent of his waking hours, she found that he nevertheless begrudged her that two percent when she wanted or needed to do other things. As she laid him in his cradle—"just for a minute, while I get my glasses from my suitcase"—he proceeded to immediately work himself into a noisy fury.

Evan was an especially alert baby and recognized me by sight extremely early. In a group he would keep his eyes on me and grin and wriggle with pleasure when I looked at him. "How bright he is!" I would crow to my husband.

"I've never seen a baby so crazy about his mother," my aunt remarked one evening when Evan was two months old. "He's going to jump right into your lap, Connie."

We were playing bridge, and as Evan had howled word of his persistent insomnia to me, I had brought him into the living room and propped him in his infant seat near me. Happy now, his eyes never left my face. Whenever I turned and spoke to him, he grinned and worked his arms and legs as if he were indeed trying to leap into my arms.

8

Aside from an easy and uncomplicated hernia operation at the age of six months, Evan had no medical problems. He was an unusually healthy baby, escaping most of the colds and "bugs" the rest of the family got. He seemed to have everything going for him, and as he grew into a plump, blond-curled cherub, we became even more impressed by signs of what we felt was great intelligence. At about seven or eight months he began to both scoot and sit up by himself, which seemed about average, but we did not base our opinion of his brightness on the timing of such ordinary functions. Rather, we noted a certain alertness in his eyes and an ardent desire to understand and relate to his surroundings.

When he was nine months old my parents and some long-time friends gathered at our house for Thanksgiving dinner. It was the cocktail hour and Evan was sitting in his stroller in our midst. Someone had just told a very funny story and we were all laughing uproariously. Evan peered from face to face, then suddenly also began to laugh. It was not a spontaneous laugh, but a kind of phony chortle. He continued to look around at each person in an obvious attempt to make them see that he, too, was "with it." Lastly, he looked at me with a pleased didn't-I-do-that-well expression on his face.

Accustomed to being carried everywhere with me or placed in whatever room I happened to be in, Evan seemed to feel that my presence was necessary to him at all times. When he was able to move by himself, he followed me from room to room, puffing determinedly behind on his tummy. The entire family might be gathered in a room, but if I slipped out, Evan soon became aware of my absence and set out to search for me.

He did not actually crawl on his hands and knees until he was about eleven months old, but he began to walk only two months later. As soon as he was able to pull himself up, I prepared to clear my tables of knickknacks as I had with the girls. I found, however, that this was not necessary. Although fascinated with the ashtrays, china boxes, and so on, Evan needed to be told "no" only once, and he would never touch a particular object again. No matter how gently the word "no" was voiced, it always hurt his feelings terribly, and the little face would crumple into tears. I had never seen a child with such an inordinate desire to avoid doing "the wrong thing."

He was fascinated by mechanical toys, locks, buckles and such things. His very favorite toy was a boxlike contraption equipped with tiny doors, knobs to pull, handles to turn and plastic gear wheels. His interest seemed to lie in figuring out just how these things worked rather than in working them once he had solved the riddle. He would experiment with a knob, intensely absorbed in determining whether it pulled, pushed or turned, and what function is served. Once he found out, though, he lost interest in that particular knob.

Evan had been given some blocks for his first birthday, and when playing alone in his room, he seemed to spend most of his time lining these up in a straight row. If anyone moved a block a fraction of an inch, Evan would dart to adjust it. One afternoon when he was around fifteen months old, I was passing his door and could have sworn I heard him saying one-two-three-four-five in baby talk. Glancing in, I saw him passing his finger down the line of blocks. Since he was saying almost no real words at this time, I thought surely my ears were deceiving me. However, several days later when I was in his room, he said distinctly enough, "One-two-three-five," and passed his finger down the row of twelve blocks, although he did not rest it on any one of them. I could see that he probably did not really understand that counting related to quantity. Still, I thought, it indicated a dawning awareness of the concept. I was even more impressed when, upon questioning the family and our baby-sitters, I found no one who could recall counting blocks with him. Obviously someone had, but at least no one had made a deliberate effort to teach him to count, and I thought him terribly clever to have picked it up. Evan never tired of making his straight rows of blocks, lining them up against his bureau and then "counting" them. I was sure this indicated an orderly mathematical mind.

If there was anything that concerned us at all, it was the ease and the frequency with which he was beginning to throw tantrums in his second year. We did not, however, consider them at all abnormal, for we realized that tantrums are quite common at this age. But it did bother us a little that we were so ineffectual in dealing with them. Very often the causes for the fits of temper seemed triflingly small: an oblong block which he could not make stand on end, for example. Sometimes we had no clue at all as to what had triggered his rage. I was beginning to think of Evan as high-strung. He was either very happy and excited or very angry and upset, but being the nervous type myself, I was not particularly surprised.

Evan's speech was coming along very slowly, but I was quite unperturbed by that. Both of the girls had been late talkers, and I knew that boys were supposed to be slower than girls. Also, the girls' high I.Q. scores later in school had emphasized to me that the age at which a child speaks does not necessarily bear any relationship to his intelligence. More likely, I thought, children felt the urge to express themselves verbally as they realized a need for it, and Evan certainly did not have a great need for it with four attentive individuals eager to grant all reasonable if unspoken desires.

Oddly, Evan was reluctant to say even those words which he knew, hoarding them like small treasures and bestowing them only upon the specially favored. He had called water "goo" since he was thirteen months or so.

11

When he was about sixteen or seventeen months, I taught him to say "water." His "wadah" was quite recognizable, but I had failed to coax him to say the word for his father. One Saturday morning when Don was still in bed, Evan toddled into the bathroom adjoining our bedroom and demanded "goo." I indicated that he must say "water." He tried "goo" five or six more times, but as I kept insisting "water!" his thirst apparently overcame his stubbornness. He hesitated, then turned, looked at his father, closed the bathroom door and only then pronounced the word "wadah." No one else would have the satisfaction of hearing him pronounce his precious word.

It was the same with the handful of other words he could say. He said them sometimes for me, rarely for his father or sisters and never for anyone else. It was true that stubbornness ran in the family, but this I thought an absurd length to which to carry it.

When Evan was about eighteen months old, Don and I went off for a weekend by ourselves. I had been reluctant to go. Evan had never been separated from me before, and I could hardly bear to contemplate his probable feeling of abandonment. But this was ridiculous, I told myself. I had taken short trips away from the girls when they had been of similar ages, and they had seemed to comprehend and adjust to the situation. Why shouldn't Evan be just as capable of understanding and adapting? I'd better be careful or I'd smother him with excessive maternal solicitude. So off we went—me to spend my time avoiding thoughts of the probably forlorn little boy at home.

When we returned we tore into the house to reunite with our children. Hugging and kissing the girls, I looked around. Where was Evan? He came strolling into the room followed by the baby-sitter. He looked past me, ignoring my excited overtures of affection. My existence

12

was simply not acknowledged. Surely he had not forgotten me, I puzzled, hurt. He was too old for that.

It was his dinner time. I put him in his high chair and gave him his meat and carrots, which he gobbled down with his fingers, still seemingly oblivious of my presence. When I offered him a cupcake, his very favorite dessert, he stared fixedly at a point just left of my head.

"Here," I said to Don, "*you* try." Don took the cupcake and Evan immediately stretched his hands toward it, accepting it delightedly from Don. It was *me*, then. Evan was angry with me. I had deserted him—forever, for all he might have known. He was going to let me suffer awhile, just as he had. For an hour or so I hovered around him like an apologetic lover waiting for forgiveness. At length Evan apparently decided I had done enough penance. Smiling with an impish twinkle in his eyes, he put his arms around my neck and squeezed. Now we would resume our relationship!

As Evan approached his second birthday, his tantrums were beginning to be more of a problem. During the day they were mostly short little storms when his desires were thwarted, but during the late afternoon he seemed to be crying constantly, often for what were, to me at least, completely obscure reasons. Again I told myself that this was not abnormal. The predinner hour is a notoriously bad time for both mothers and small children.

As an infant Evan had had a bottle at eleven or twelve o'clock at night, and he had never gotten over "fussing" at this time. Sometimes he didn't quite wake up, but more often he did, and as he went into his third year we seemed to have more trouble soothing him back to sleep.

He was saying quite a few words now and fairly clearly, but he did not use sentences or even phrases, with the exception of "want some——"cookie, water or whatever.

He had a disconcerting habit of echoing what we said to him without any apparent attempt to understand it. Thus I might say "Close the door" and he would look blankly at me and repeat "Close the door." I felt that he just did not want to be bothered.

I congratulated myself that I was so calm about this slowness in speech. As a very young mother with the girls, I probably would have been getting rather upset, I thought. Now, however, experience told me that as I knew he had a good mind, could hear well, could speak clearly enough when he desired, there was nothing left to be alarmed over.

I was stunned one evening when Don suddenly asked, "Is he all right?" I assumed he was questioning Evan's mental capacity, and I sputtered indignantly, "All right? All right! Of course he's all right! How many children have the reasoning ability that we see in him? How many babies are starting to count at fifteen months?" Further words failed me.

Apparently reassured by my maternal instinct, Don did not pursue it, but I felt shaken. It disturbed me to realize that the only thing that had really surprised me was that one so close should doubt that Evan was "all right." Yes, Evan's limited speech and lack of understanding of it might certainly lead outsiders to think him slow. Lately, I had found myself explaining to people who were not asking that Evan didn't say much because he just didn't feel the necessity of it. Was my maternal pride blinding me to what others might be seeing? I tried hard to think objectively. No, I couldn't believe it! I had watched the wheels in that little mind turning, solving problems that took a good reasoning ability. Impossible that a subaverage intellect could operate in that way! In my mind as well as my heart, I was certain that Evan was of not only normal but superior intelligence. Certain. Yes! But why was I still uneasy?

14

In September 1967, when Evan was two years and seven months, I took him to the pediatrician for a routine checkup. Since we had changed pediatricians the winter before, this was only the second time this doctor had seen Evan.

"He's a beautiful boy," said the doctor, "but he's very immature. He shouldn't be behaving like this." Evan had fought the examination every step of the way, finally dissolving into frightened tears. He of course had not responded to the doctor's attempts to converse with him.

"You're spoiling him," the doctor continued. "You and his daddy and sisters probably wait on him hand and foot and give him whatever he wants. He just has no incentive to assert his independence. It's too much fun being a baby. Don't make things so easy for him. Make him ask for what he wants, and don't give it to him unless he does. He can ask and he can understand, too. In fact, he understands every word I'm saying right now. Don't think he doesn't!" and he grinned at Evan.

I looked doubiously at my son. Understand every word? Did he? I just really could not quite believe that. Should he be able to? I felt that the doctor was not only assuming but expecting a lot. Perhaps my instincts were betraying me, though. Maybe Evan did understand all that we said and was playing a game in an effort to hold on to his babyhood.

On the whole I felt rather relieved. The pediatrician seemed to see Evan's slowness as I did—a refusal rather than an inability to make more of an effort toward growing up. I, too, had thought that this refusal was rooted in a sort of supersecurity. Evan was surrounded entirely by affectionate and solicitous parents and older sisters. There were no little ones to compete with.

I pondered upon this probability that our very family

15

structure was holding Evan back. The problem was what to do about it. The somewhat unusual age grouping of our children was unchangeable. What really significant change could we make? We were not ignorant, after all, and had not been so carried away by affection that we were spoiling Evan blindly. We put restraints on his behavior; there were things he was not allowed to do or to play with. We mainly ignored his tantrums or put him in his room until he was finished, and the girls were not allowed to comfort him during these temper storms. The only thing we could really do differently was to insist that he ask for whatever he wanted, for we had not really made a point of this. But was this one change enough to make a great difference, I wondered?

I voiced my reflections to the pediatrician. "Do you have any other suggestions that would help him along?" I asked him.

"Nursery school!" he said emphatically, as if he had been coming to that.

This had crossed my mind but I had dismissed it because of one seemingly insurmountable difficulty. "But Evan isn't toilet trained. They don't take children in diapers, do they?"

"No, that's right, they don't!" remembered the doctor, snapping his fingers. "Well, bring him back in four months, and if he hasn't started to make more progress, we'll think about a special nursery school." Ending the interview, he briskly left the room.

A *special* nursery school! I thought, getting Evan's clothes on. What did he mean by that?

Heading home in the car, I contemplated our problem. I was concerned but not really deeply worried. It was simply a matter of finding a proper solution, and we would find one, that was all. Evan was not going to turn into a spoiled, dependent sissy, because we would not allow it to happen. We loved him far too much for that.

We would do whatever was necessary. There must be *someplace* that would take children in diapers, I thought.

"Immature? Meaning just what exactly?" asked Don slowly when I told him that evening. I knew he was asking if the doctor thought Evan was mentally slow.

"It's just an emotional or social thing," I hurried to explain. "We both know there's nothing wrong with his mind. He's terribly intelligent. In fact, perhaps that's part of the trouble. He's smart enough to know he can get by without doing some of these things." I was developing a habit of blaming Evan's intelligence for his faults.

I told Don of the nursery school idea and we agreed that we must attempt to find a place that would take damp children. Waiting four months for something Evan needed now was unthinkable.

I called a friend who lived across the street and asked her about the nursery school she had sent her children to. She was full of enthusiasm over the place, and thought it had particularly helped her son's development. A little embarrassed, I asked the all-important question: Did they take children in diapers? She didn't know, but thought they might since they had some quite tiny children.

At eight-thirty the next morning I called the school. I explained to the lady who answered the telephone that our pediatrician had recommended nursery school for our son and asked her if they had a place for a two-and-a-half-year-old. When she said they did, I took a deep breath and asked her if they took children who were not toilet trained. Well, they *liked* them to be trained, but if I would put him in training pants plus plastic pants, and would work with him at home, they would accept him. I restrained myself from letting out a whoop. The lady suggested I bring Evan down for a visit.

In less than an hour Evan and I were sitting on tiny

17

chairs, watching a group of two-year-olds smear paint on paper, faces, smocks. Their teacher, a patient woman called "Miss Addy" (who, I learned later, was married and had three children), was young looking, and while not quite pretty, had a special kind of attractiveness. Her eyes sparkled with enthusiasm, and I could see that she was truly fond of these children.

Delighted with what I saw, I went to the office with "Miss Bonnie" and arranged for Evan to spend Monday, Tuesday and Thursday mornings at the school. Having obtained the necessary health forms, we drove straight to the doctor's office to have them filled out and signed. I was eager to get Evan started on his new "program of reform." Too, I knew there would be a painful adjustment to make, and I wanted to get it over with.

There was no way in which I could explain to Evan what was going to happen, so it was a completely unprepared and unsuspecting child I presented to the little school the next morning. I had steeled myself for the inevitable tears, but nothing could have prepared me for the scene that took place. All attempts to gently handle the parting failed, so he was half-carried, half-dragged away from me—his little arms stretched vainly toward me, his heartrending cries ringing through the building. I could not have felt more like a traitor if I had just sold him. Unable to hold back my own tears, I rushed home to spend my newfound free time pacing, crying, smoking and watching the clock. The real agony was that there had been no way of making him understand that I would be back to reclaim him, and I tormented myself with the image of my pathetic little boy, his heart breaking because he thought his mother had deserted him forever and ever.

With what I thought was really admirable self-restraint, I lasted almost the entire three hours, appearing only twenty minutes early to reunite with my child. Evan was glad to see me but seemed to have been playing

18

calmly enough. Miss Addy thought he had settled down quite well. The very fact that the experience had been such a ghastly ordeal for both of us showed me how much Evan needed these short flights from the nest. Knowing that the worst was over, I felt optimistic and confident that we were on the right course.

For two more mornings our partings were tearful, but there was no panic. Evan now understood that he was only going to spend the morning at school, that Mama would return to take him home again. By the second week he was arriving at school with a smile, and by the third, he was tugging at my hand and hurrying me along on the way in. He obviously was at home in the class now, and Don and I felt that he had taken the first big step toward growing up.

On the Monday of Evan's fourth week at school, Don was home for the morning. Anxious to see the nursery school, he picked Evan up at noon. The moment they returned home, Evan threw himself on the floor and began to tantrum. I looked questioningly at Don but he shrugged his shoulders, equally puzzled. Evan continued to vent his anger through lunch, and he spent much of the afternoon in fits of enraged crying.

On Tuesday morning he was still very cranky and fussy but I drove him to school, hoping his mood would brighten. On entering the classroom he ran to get his favorite toy, and I left, relieved that he seemed his usual self. Upon returning at eleven-thirty, however, I could hear him screaming before I even got out of the car.

"He must be tired," Miss Bonnie told me. "He's been keeping this up all morning." I carried the unhappy little boy to the car and drove him home, but his anger seemed to be growing. At home I tried to give him lunch. He pushed it away, so I put him in his room for a nap. I was relieved when he fell into an exhausted sleep. Like Miss Bonnie, I thought his problem must be fatigue, but when later he woke up and resumed crying almost immediately, I began to feel real concern. I knew he was not ill. There was no doubt that this was anger, not pain. I was completely in the dark as to the cause of his fury. All efforts to soothe him failed utterly; my helplessness added to my bewildered frustration.

On Wednesday Evan awoke late. The cries I was listening for started as if there had been no interruption. Frightened now, I spent the morning holding him, rocking him, making every effort to comfort him. He would occasionally fall asleep for a few minutes, then, with renewed strength, build to a new momentum. Around noon, as his screams started to build to a frightening crescendo, my mind was suddenly possessed by what I thought was a terrifying certainty. Evan was mentally ill!

Years before, forgotten until now, I had read an account of a little boy who was schizophrenic and whose symptoms had begun in exactly this manner. I burst into tears. Seeing this, Evan began to throw his head from side to side, and I struggled to control myself. Kissing him, I put him in his bed and telephoned Don, sobbing that he must come home, something was terribly wrong with Evan. Strengthened by the sound of Don's voice and the knowledge that he would be home shortly, I rested the receiver in its cradle, composing myself before I dialed the pediatrician.

The receptionist's voice was wary as I told her I must speak to the doctor as soon as possible. She guarded his calls like a dragon at the castle moat. Just what was my problem? I explained that my little boy was in his third day of almost steady tantrumming and, my voice beginning to shake again, I said I was sure that he had gone over the brink of sanity. Her voice was crisp and professional. The doctor was examining a patient now but if I would leave my number she would have him call.

"Please be sure he calls just as soon as he can. I'm really frightened," I begged.

20

Evan had finally fallen into a deep sleep. The house was silent as I sat by the telephone, willing it to ring. When Don arrived half an hour later, the doctor still had not called. Don was not quite ready to agree that Evan had lost his sanity, but he was gravely concerned. He dialed the pediatrician's office.

The doctor was out to lunch, he was told blandly. Furious, Don told the "dragon" with as much restraint as he could muster that we had been counting on speaking to the doctor right away. It was in the nature of an emergency and to please have him call the moment he was back from lunch.

Two hours later the doctor finally returned our call. After hearing a brief account of Evan's behavior, he told us to bring him into the office. By this time Evan had awakened, still crying but with little strength. As we drove to the doctor's office, he was calm and quiet for the first time in days. Don and I exchanged weak smiles. The little rascal was going to make us look like a pair of hysterical idiots. By the time the doctor greeted us in the examination room, Evan was his usual self, smiling and inspecting the premises with interest. Conscious that we probably looked rather silly, Don and I were only a little less worried. Giving the doctor a detailed account of the past three days, I asked him if a normal child could behave in this fashion.

The doctor's face was grave, but his words were reassuring. Yes, sometimes they did, even occasionally giving themselves concussions by banging their heads against walls. This type of behavior did not necessarily indicate any abnormality. He gave Evan a brief examination.

"He certainly seems all right. There's nothing physically the matter. I'm going to prescribe phenobarbital for a couple of weeks. Twice a day!" He wrote the prescription.

21

"What could have caused this, Doctor?" asked my husband.

The doctor shrugged. "You'll probably never know. Could be a nightmare, something else that frightened him. Have there been any changes in his life lately?"

"Well, of course, he's been going to nursery school for the last few weeks," I said, a little surprised that he didn't remember.

"I'd say cut out the school, then."

I was dismayed. "But he has adjusted so well and seems so happy there now! I really don't think it's the school that caused this, and it seems to be doing him so much good. I'd hate to give it up!"

The doctor nodded. "All right, if he seems to be happy about it, then keep him there. Give him the phenobarbital for a couple of weeks and call me if he hasn't settled down by that time. Otherwise, I'll see this young man in four months!"

Once more in the car, unspeakably relieved, Don and I discussed the mystery that had brought on the trauma. It was a nightmare, we decided. Lately, when Evan had awakened late at night crying, he was often obviously afraid of something. His frightened eyes would be fastened on the window as if he saw something terrifying there; I had even gone to look several times. I had been puzzled because he had never been told frightening stories, indeed, could not have understood them. Moreover, in the light of the day, he seemed to have very little fear of anything.

Now I turned to study the little figure kneeling on the back seat of the car, absorbed in the passing landscape. The handsome features were untroubled. Whatever had called forth such terrible rage was, for the moment, forgotten.

What bogeyman threatened my son, I wondered. If only he could tell me!

22

The following March I drove Evan toward the pediatrician's office feeling a trifle guilty. It had been closer to five months than four since our last frantic visit. The winter had passed swiftly and so pleasantly that our fright had all but been forgotten. The phenobarbital had calmed Evan down immediately and there had been no repetition of the terrible, uninterrupted tantrumming. In fact, his behavior had returned so quickly and completely to normal that I had taken him off the barbiturate a few days early. He did not awaken so often at night now, and although he still threw a tantrum at the drop of a hat, we accepted this as one of the inevitable hardships of disciplining a strong-willed, slightly spoiled family "baby."

Don and I were tremendously pleased with Evan's adjustment at nursery school. Although still very much his mother's boy, he accepted these short separations from me naturally and seemed to enjoy this other part of his life. Actually, he seemed much more mature about this than some of his small classmates, who would occasionally cling tearfully to their mothers in the morning. Evan did not play with the other children, but this was not very unusual at his age. Many of the others played independently also.

I knew that Evan was fond of Miss Addy and considered her the most important person in his world, outside of his family. He took for granted her hugs and kisses as his natural due. One day, when Miss Addy had returned after a two-week absence, she greeted me at noon with a particularly happy smile lighting her face.

"You know," she said, "Evan has never sought out affection from me as the others do. He just always behaved as if he gets all the affection he needs at home and doesn't require any more. This morning, though,

23

when we sat around the table, each telling our name, Evan kept staring at me. Suddenly he got up and came around the table, put his arms around my neck and gave me a squeeze. Then he went back to his place and sat down."

Miss Addy was genuinely touched at this spontaneous demonstration of the little boy's love, and I was happy that Evan had offered it to her. It was true, I thought. Evan was constantly being cuddled and kissed, and he regarded such expressions of affection as he did the air he breathed.

On another occasion Miss Addy told me delightedly that Evan had hit another little boy. "I was just so glad!" she exclaimed. "Usually Evan just shrugs when another child snatches a toy from him—not that he is afraid of the others, he just doesn't seem to care. This morning, though, when another little boy tried to take Evan's favorite pull toy, he put up a fight!"

Some mornings Evan did not deign to participate in all of the activities with the rest of the class, but he would usually sit quietly and watch. This we took as just another quirk of an independent spirit accustomed to having its own way. Miss Addy was noticing what we had already discovered at home—Evan's fascination with music. He had an instinctive sense of rhythm, clapping his hands in perfect time. For Christmas and for his birthday in February, we gave him mostly musical toys. These were the only toys that really excited his interest anymore. I began to wonder if perhaps we were witnessing the first signs of genius. Evan certainly had the intense type of personality that, from all I had read, so often went with a gifted mentality. There was no calm middleground in his moods. When he was happy he was excited, often running back and forth clapping his hands. When he was unhappy he was angry and howling with rage.

24

I was disappointed that I had been unsuccessful in my attempts to read to him. He simply did not seem to be able to sit still and concentrate long enough. I realized that he could not understand a story as yet, but I had begun to read to the girls in their second year and they had enjoyed it even when their understanding was still vague. I was confused as to just how much speech Evan could really understand. Surely more than he let on. He could repeat almost any word or phrase. Yet he used only single words and a couple of short phrases, meaningfully, to express what he had to.

Another facet of this unconventional personality was a great emphasis on ritual. Evan insisted that the smallest details of his daily routine be conducted in precisely the same way. If one deviated in the least from the pattern, he exploded with rage. The girls, like most small children, had demanded a certain amount of ritual, so I was puzzled only by the degree of importance Evan placed on this sameness in routine, and the lengths to which he carried it.

He was oddly interested in smells. When he encountered anything for the first time—be it food, a toy, furniture, whatever—the first thing he did was to put his nose to it and sniff. I could not remember the girls having done this except with new foods that apparently looked suspiciously unappetizing.

Simply, Evan was not an ordinary little boy. He marched to the beat of a different drum. I mentioned to Don that we would have to be very careful in planning Evan's education. He was quite possibly brilliant, and that precariously balanced personality of the highly intelligent would have to be carefully handled.

As we approached the doctor's office now, however, my thoughts were not on the future but on the present. Evan was three years old, and so far my attempts to toilet

25

train him had been an utter flop. I hoped the doctor would have a few tips for me. I was beginning to lose my confidence in being a competent mother.

"Are you still giving him phenobarbital?" the pediatrician asked as he finished examining Evan.

"Why, no!" I answered, amazed. Surely the man did not think I'd been feeding the child barbiturates for almost five months!

The doctor lifted Evan to the floor, then sat down, absently rolling his pencil over and over in his two hands. "Evan is strange." He paused and looked across the table at me.

"Yes," I agreed, not without a touch of pride. "He is that!" No commonplace, run-of-the-mill child, mine!

The doctor fixed his eyes once more upon his pencil. "I can't put my finger on it, whether it's a nervous thing or he's mentally retarded or something else, but he doesn't seem normal. I'm sure you and your husband have probably noticed something. I may be wrong, I hope so. But I think we should start keeping the possibility of an abnormality in mind."

The doctor kept talking but I did not hear him. I sat paralyzed, the words "mentally retarded" reverberating, bouncing back and forth off the walls of my mind as in an echo chamber. Mentally retarded! Mentally retarded!

The doctor was rising and I realized that he was about to leave.

"He can count to ten!" My words detained him for a moment. "Could he count to ten if he were retarded?" Wildly searching my mind for some proof of Evan's intelligence, I fastened upon this accomplishment.

"Yes, yes he could." The doctor nodded vigorously, unimpressed. "Memory rote, that doesn't indicate intelligence."

"But he *reasons* so well. I can see that. I've watched him figure things out which he has no prior knowledge of!"

26

But the busy pediatrician could spare no more time. "We'll wait and see," he threw over his shoulder, and as he closed the door behind him, I found myself alone with Evan in the tiny cell of a room.

Dazed with shock, I forced my mind to focus on the practical details of getting home. Forced my hands to dress Evan, forced my feet to make their way to the front desk, paid the bill—all as if the world had not just suddenly exploded.

Guiding the car into the late afternoon traffic, I was dimly aware that I was sobbing aloud. My darling, beautiful baby. Was it possible? Mentally retarded? *Dear God,* was it possible? No, no, no, *no!*

"It's all right, darling," I said aloud to the happily innocent child. "It's all right."

At home I paced the floor, waiting for Don, trying to organize the chaos of my mind. I had instinctively felt, from the time Evan was a few weeks old, that he was of superior intelligence. Could I possibly be that wrong? Perhaps, to an extent. Maternal love might make an average child seem superior—but a retarded child? Surely I could not be that blind!

We had to find out!

For the first time I became aware that the pediatrician had mentioned other possibilities. ". . . A nervous thing . . . something else . . ." The vagueness of these words was comforting. It left the door open for any one of a multitude of relatively minor problems. But what? We had to find out, I thought again. If there was something wrong with Evan we had to know now. Wait and see? We could not possibly live with such a doubt. I began to regain command of myself as my mind concentrated on a course of action. We would take Evan somewhere to be tested. We would do it immediately.

When Don got home I told him what the doctor had said and then quickly went on to my plan. "I want to take

Evan someplace where he can be thoroughly tested. I want to find out right now if there is anything wrong, and if so, what!"

"Absolutely!" Don agreed. He was already looking for the pediatrician's telephone number.

The doctor seemed to approve of our decision to have Evan tested right away, and told us to call Orange County Children's Hospital and make an appointment with Dr. Thomas Ward, a psychologist there. Under Don's worried questioning, the pediatrician confessed that he had probably been a little careless in his use of the term "mentally retarded."

That was it then. I would call for an appointment with Dr. Ward the first thing in the morning. After that there would be nothing to do but wait and see what the tests showed. Just wait, Don and I agreed. Carry on as usual until we knew something definite.

Don and I were especially full of small talk at dinner that evening, and after the children were in bed, we watched television, trying hard to absorb ourselves in the predicaments of fictional characters. After an endless evening I kissed Don and went to get ready for bed. I undressed slowly, then scrubbed my teeth as if their care was my greatest concern. Unable to stall any longer, I finally turned off the light and got into bed. I would scrub the kitchen floor tomorrow, I thought. Then, turning my face toward my pillow, I cried as I never had before.

On the morning of our appointment with Dr. Ward, I arose early, for we were scheduled to see him at nine o'clock and we wanted to allow half an hour to get there. All mothers know that the washing and dressing of a small child is done immediately before taking him anywhere, leaving him no time to undo her handiwork. So at eight-thirty I had just finished buttoning Evan into a blue and white checked sunsuit. Cindy and Wendy, innocent of our errand, had already left for the school bus, and Don, with an impatient eye on his watch, was watching me dress Evan.

We were nervous but optimistic about the test. In the ten days since my traumatic visit to the pediatrician, Don and I had regained our equilibrium and confidence in our own judgment. Yes, it was quite possible that Evan had some minor problem that needed correcting. We would simply find out what it was and see that it was corrected, that was all. Like most parents, we had had such things before. Cindy's teeth had needed straightening. Wendy's feet had called for minor adjustments. Evan himself had had a hernia that had required surgery. It was possible that he had some slight hearing defect that was slowing up his speech. Or, the pediatrician had mentioned "a nervous problem." Perhaps Evan was just unusually nervous and needed a little careful handling and maybe a tranquilizer for a while.

In any event, whatever the problem we were certain that mental retardation was out of the question. After our initial stunned reaction to the very suggestion of such a thing, Don and I tried hard to take an objective look at Evan. We found ourselves giving him things to do which demanded a good reasoning ability, and as we watched him methodically solve the problems, we were reassured.

"Miss Addy" had agreed with us. We had told her of the forthcoming examination; even confided that the pediatrician had mentioned the term "mentally retarded." We asked her to think carefully and give us a brief report before the test.

Evan was certainly different, she had decided. He was not able to do many of the things that other children did, but when it came to anything that required basic inductive reasoning, he was way out in front of them. For example, on a walk the class had come to a gate they had never seen before. The other children pushed at it and when it didn't give, continued to push. Evan, however, after one push, examined the gate, found the latch, then proceeded to figure out how it worked. This, Miss Addy said, was typical. The other children would sometimes learn to do something by watching Evan figure it out first. In general activities, however, such as drawing, cutting and clay, Evan did not perform as the other children, nor did he seem very interested in doing so. In fact, some mornings he did not care to participate at all and would sit at the side of the room and simply watch. As for his behavior with the other children, he paid very little attention to them. Yes, he was different, Miss Addy had concluded, and he was puzzling, but not at all like any retarded children she had seen.

The hospital had sent us a lengthy questionnaire to fill out on Evan's birth and development. The questions themselves, as well as the lack of anything radically deviant from the norm in our own answers, had further reinforced our feeling that nothing could be terribly wrong.

Now I hurriedly combed Evan's softly curling blond hair into place, enjoying as always, the picture he made. ("Handsome blond boy," would be the first words in the psychologist's report.) Evan knew by our preparations that we were going someplace, and the excitement of an unexpected adventure, together with the blue and white

30

sunsuit, made his eyes seem larger and bluer than ever.

My eyes met Don's and we smiled together knowing we were sharing a thought. There could not be very much wrong. It was too perfect a picture. And so we rushed away, to find out if our son had a problem of any kind, and if so, what was needed to correct it. When we returned, it was with the knowledge that our little boy had been mysteriously, inexplicably injured, and as a result, had been left cruelly handicapped.

31

During the following weeks I would move as a dreamer who knows she is dreaming. This wasn't happening. Not really. I would wake up. Some inner part of me took command, guiding my actions and leading me to grasp the full reality of Evan's predicament. With an effort at playing the detached researcher, I would read everything I could lay hands on (which was appallingly little) that would help me to understand my son's puzzling and complicated disorder.

*Neurologically handicapped,* Dr. Ward had said. *Brain-damaged. Severe developmental aphasia, and probable visuo-motor impairment.*

I was to find that in order to benefit from the material available on the subject, I must myself act as interpreter and coordinator of the variously worded reports. While there were some different theories concerning the disorder, I would determine that the majority of physicians, psychologists and educators specializing in the field were in general agreement. Often, what seemed to be different theories were only different approaches or different areas of emphasis. The field was young, very young, and as yet there was no one, universally given explanation.

Dr. Ward told us that as little as ten years before, Evan's true problem would probably have gone undiagnosed. He would simply have been pronounced mentally retarded and treated accordingly. Now, although the disorder was gaining recognition, there were as yet no real answers to it, nor was it fully understood. The experts themselves were in the process of learning.

In my subsequent searchings I found the newness of the field graphically demonstrated by the inconsistency of the terminology. According to what I had been reading, Evan was neurologically handicapped (N.H.), brain-damaged, brain-injured, or he suffered from "minimal brain dysfunction." Because his most devastating handicap was aphasia, he might be labeled simply "aphasic" and described as if this were the whole of his problem. Developmental aphasia is the inability to speak and/or to understand speech.

Dr. Ward told us that Evan most definitely had the latter disorder; that is, he had *receptive* aphasia. Although there was probably nothing wrong with his hearing itself, the language center of his brain was unable to properly interpret the words it received through the nerves from the ear. Thus, most of the language that Evan heard was a jumble of meaningless sounds. It was almost impossible to ascertain whether or not he had *expressive* aphasia. This would have been where his brain knew the words he wanted to say but was unable to send the proper message to his tongue. Evan could certainly say some words quite clearly, but expressive aphasia could manifest itself in more subtle ways, such as an inability to put words in their proper order in sentences. If you do not understand French you cannot speak it, and there was no way to determine if Evan's speech deficiency was caused by anything more than his lack of knowledge of it.

Just as the nerves from Evan's ears did not send the proper communications to his brain, so Dr. Ward was fairly certain that the nerves from his eyes similarly garbled messages. Although Evan's eyesight was probably all right, by the time his brain received visual images they were distorted and inaccurate. His brain did not correctly *interpret* what he saw. If Evan had been older, and not so overwhelmingly aphasic, he might have been described as *dyslectic* (having dyslexia—difficulty in learning to read). The dyslectic child may *disassociate;* that is, fail to see things in their proper relationships. Whereas we may see the letter *H,* he may see three disconnected and unrelated lines. Although this problem would extend to

34

all that the child sees, it usually does not become obvious until he is in school and is trying to learn to read.

*Figure-background reversal* is another characteristic of the dyslectic child. This is where background stimuli take precedence over a foreground stimulus. Thus, the child may find it difficult to concentrate on a single word on a page or an object in a room, as all the background words or objects "jump out" at him. Or he may have another type of reversal problem where he lacks a normal awareness of "forward" and "backward" and is unable to differentiate between the letters *d* and *b*, or the words *tab* and *bat*.

Dr. Ward said that he felt Evan had at least some motor impairment, although, since his severe receptive aphasia precluded his understanding of instructions, it was difficult to ascertain the extent of it. *Gross* motor impairment is fairly obvious; indeed, it usually shows up in babyhood, when the child has difficulty learning to sit, crawl, walk, etc. A child, however, might appear to be fairly well coordinated but have difficulty with such *fine* motor skills as tying, buttoning, handwriting, etc. Evan seemed unable to string beads for Dr. Ward, but then, the psychologist could not be certain that Evan even understood what he was supposed to do.

I would later determine from my reading that disassociation, figure-background reversal, and gross and/or fine motor impairment are apparently connected with the absence of or lag in the natural development of a child's laterality. Laterality is the awareness of the two sides of the body and the difference between them. If Evan had difficulty in differentiating between the two sides of his own body, he would naturally have trouble recognizing the relationship of objects to himself and to each other; thus, visuo-motor problems.

I would find *perseveration* to be a term often associated with neurologically handicapped children, and would

35

immediately recognize the manifestations of this symptom. The word is closely related to "perseverance," but whereas the latter is an admirable trait, perseveration shackles the mind. It is the inability to shift from one mental activity to another. The mind gets "stuck" in one place, as a phonograph needle does in a crack on a record. I thought of Evan "counting" his row of blocks over and over and over. A related type of perseverative behavior is an abnormal insistence upon apparently meaningless patterns in routine functions. So much for Evan's "rituals."

I would learn that hyperactivity is so very often a symptom of the neurologically handicapped child, that such children are frequently called simply "hyperactive" or "hyperkinetic." There are two types of hyperactivity, and a child may have either or both. There is sensory hyperactivity, in which the child responds to irrelevant stimuli; and motor hyperactivity, where the child is constantly touching and meddling with everything in sight. Evan seemed to have the former type, for he was abnormally distractible.

The further my investigations took me, the more I realized that there was no such thing as a typical neurologically handicapped child, which was perhaps why the material on the subject so often seemed just off the mark. One could simply not describe the disorder as one could a case of measles. The symptoms and combinations, and the severity of symptoms, varied radically from child to child. The reading proved generally informative, but it would not tell me nearly enough about *Evan's* handicap.

Dr. Ward warned us that neurologically handicapped children virtually always have or are on their way to developing emotional problems. This was a result of the poor self-image the child would inevitably develop when he saw that he could not perform as others did.

The psychologist did not overwhelm us with long technical details, but instead offered us various analogies to convey Evan's predicament to us. The ear and the brain—like two telephones in working order, but the wires between were damaged, garbling the messages. Same with the eye and the brain. Knowing that we, like most parents who hear this diagnosis for the first time, were quite in the dark regarding the strange disorder, he offered us unhurried silences, to absorb the meaning of what we had just heard, and the opportunity to ask the questions that formed in our minds.

"This doesn't mean that Evan is mentally retarded, does it, Dr. Ward?" I phrased the question in the negative as if to assure a negative reply. This had been the term that had given us our initial fright; surely Evan's mental ability was the only really important thing! Why had Dr. Ward not mentioned it?

The psychologist spoke carefully. "I don't know. *Inside* his intellect may be normal, but there is no way of ascertaining this. You see, that part of his brain which thinks and reasons may be undamaged and quite normal, but it is *locked up*. There is simply no way of getting to it right now. Let us assume that inwardly he does have normal intelligence. All of what he hears is garbled—meaningless. What he sees is distorted too. By the time sounds and images reach this inner part of the brain, none of it makes any sense. He isn't receiving any meaningful messages. He cannot acquire knowledge. That part of the brain which could think normally if information could get to it is cut off—imprisoned, really. It can't function and grow. Already, Evan has lost ground. He could not pass the intelligence test. So, in answer to your question, I just don't know whether Evan's inner intellect is normal or not, but . . ."

But it doesn't matter, I inwardly finished for him. He

37

didn't need to go on. The picture was all too clear. Better if Evan had no intelligence at all, than to have it withering and dying inside. *My God!*

"What can we do?" asked Don. "There must be some sort of treatment."

"He will have speech therapy. What the therapist will do is to try to find a *key* to communicating with him. If this can be done, then Evan can begin learning. Even then, though, it would be hard to get enough through to him to prevent him from growing up to be retarded. I'm afraid the outlook is not at all hopeful when the handicap is this severe."

"I suppose he'll have to go to special schools?" Don remarked questioningly. This would have seemed a foregone conclusion, under the circumstances, but it all seemed so very unreal.

"Definitely." Dr. Ward nodded vehemently as if to help us to absorb our situation.

"What could have caused this—'damage'?" I asked.

Dr. Ward had been waiting for that, and he shot me a sudden penetrating look. "It was an accident," he said with deliberate emphasis. "We don't know what causes it. It was probably something that happened during the pregnancy, perhaps a virus that you were not even aware you had. Whatever it was, you probably could not have prevented it had you known of it."

I understood what he was telling me, that I must not blame myself, add guilt to my grief. And I was grateful, for I knew there would be times when I would need to remember those words. All the same, for the first time that morning, my eyes filled with tears and Don suddenly whipped out his sunglasses and put them on in the quietly lit room. We were feeling the same emotion: not guilt, but a frustrated, grief-stricken anger. We had lain unsuspecting while an unseen thing had come as a thief in the night and robbed our beautiful, perfect child of his rightful possession. Had I had a terrible accident or disease while carrying Evan, or a dangerous and complicated delivery, it would have been easier to understand, possibly to accept.

We talked some more of practical procedural matters: additional tests Evan should have—neurological examination, hearing test, speech evaluation, electroencephalograph—where we might take him for therapy and the possibilities of medication. There were certain drugs that were sometimes helpful to neurologically handicapped children. Although stimulants, they acted as tranquilizers upon some of these children and, even more, seemed to stimulate certain nerves so that they could learn more easily. We must find a medication for Evan, I thought, a small hope beginning to take root.

"You have to sort of spoil him," Dr. Ward told us, speaking of the behavioral problems that invariably accompanied the disorder. Don and I smiled faintly at each other. To think we had worried about spoiling Evan!

Neither Don nor I could ever clearly remember the end of the consultation nor leaving the hospital. It was the beginning of a different life—the end, so we thought, of a life that included happiness.

The following several weeks were the most difficult that Don and I had ever experienced. This was our "period of adjustment." Ironically, I recalled the idiotic statement I had once made to Don shortly before Evan's birth, "The one thing I really don't think I could go through is something really terrible happening to one of my children—death or some tragic defect."

What do we mean when we say we "cannot go through" such a situation? I had been given no alternative; I *had* to go through it and, further, go through it *well.* The one whose sufferings, or probable future sufferings, were causing me so much sorrow, was trustingly holding my hand, confident that I knew where I was going and would lead him there safely. Therefore, I not only had to hold myself together, but much more; indeed, I had to equip myself with all that might be required to lead him safely.

Grief, like pain, is an intensely personal thing. People can share love, happiness, pride. But one grieves alone. The knowledge that one's own sorrow will only confirm and intensify another's makes us stand apart, helpless to comfort. Thus, Don and I each sought within ourselves for some way to bear that which seemed unbearable.

Our little boy could not be like other little boys. Someday he must suffer the pain of that realization. Worst of all, his handicap was capable of barring him forever from the world of the normal. Born bright and intelligent (for I was still certain of this), Evan could be trapped in the limited world of the retarded.

I dared not cry for I knew I would not know how to stop. Nor could I allow myself to dwell on the dangers of Evan's predicament. I had to find a solution first, some weapon with which to arm myself before I could look the enemy in the eye.

41

Those closest to us must be told. There was no point in putting it off. So, assuming an air of bright confidence which impressed no one, Don and I endeavored to break gently the news for which everyone was so unprepared. I called my parents, who lived in a distant city, the afternoon following our visit to Dr. Ward. I talked with my mother and found that she knew a little about neurologically handicapped children, making my task a bit easier. She was calm and encouraging. That evening Don called his mother, who also lived in another town, and like ourselves she had almost no knowledge of the disorder.

It was not until the following evening, after numerous mental rehearsals, that I felt ready to tell Cindy and Wendy. I called them to the kitchen as I was preparing dinner, thinking rather illogically that somehow the very ordinary sight of me aproned, stirring a pot on the stove, would make my words less frightening. I attempted to explain Evan's trouble in words they could understand. I said nothing of the possible implications for the future, only that he would have to have a great deal of special training to help him learn as others do.

The girls listened silently, then, after a question or two, abruptly left the room. When I called them later for dinner, they appeared again, quiet and red-eyed. Our dinner was interrupted by the ring of the telephone. It was Don's mother. Disturbed and upset, she had gone to talk with her own doctor, who was a personal friend of hers. He had discussed with her the nature of Evan's disorder, clearing up much of her confusion. Finally, Mother had asked him, "If it were your son, to whom in the whole state of California would you take him?"

Unhesitatingly, the doctor replied, "I'd take him to Dr. Merl Carson. He's one of the finest specialists in this field in the country."

Mother was obviously excited. It had turned out, she went on, that this man who was a pediatric neurologist

42

was in our own area. Children's Hospital, her doctor had said. She had assumed he was speaking of the one in Los Angeles.

Eagerly, Don and I called our pediatrician. Absolutely, the pediatrician agreed enthusiastically. There was no finer physician than Dr. Carson. No, he was not in Los Angeles. He was the medical director of Children's Hospital of Orange County, the very place we had just been!

It was difficult to wait until the next morning when I could call for an appointment with the noted specialist, but my impatience was only a prelude to what promised to be a lesson in the art of waiting. Dr. Carson was out of the state and would not return until June. I managed, however, to get an appointment with him for the week following his return. Weeks and weeks of waiting! How could we endure it?

Our lives instantly became focused upon this one single event. Nothing else we did had any meaning in itself. Our activities were merely a means of passing the time. I hardly knew just what our appointment with Dr. Carson meant to me. I did not really expect a different diagnosis. I respected Dr. Ward and was certain that he was right. Nor did I expect a magic solution to the problem. Had there been one, Dr. Ward would have known of it. It was, I suppose, confirmation I needed—a final dispelling of any lingering doubts—to turn my feeling of unreality into acceptance so that I could go on from there.

A neurological examination was important anyway. Dr. Ward had mentioned it. But the fact that it was to be done by someone so highly thought of in the profession gave the event the importance needed to put an end to conjecture.

I filled my days with busy activity—dusting, vacuuming, sewing, baking—and as I worked I tried to organize my thoughts, to analyze Evan's problem and to achieve an intelligent understanding of it. Aphasia—I knew something of this in connection with stroke or accident victims. I had usually thought of it as mainly an expressive problem, where the afflicted person could think the words he wanted to say but was unable to express them verbally. This impression did not fit Evan. If he knew the term for an object he usually had no trouble saying it, in reasonably clear three-year-old language—"ball," "school," "Mama." He did speak some gibberish, but this seemed to be when he had no idea of the words he wanted to use. He constantly repeated phrases after us. His trouble seemed to be that he did not understand the meaning of most words that we said or even some of the words that he said, particularly when he was repeating. He did, however, know the meaning of many words. When we whispered "cake," there was no doubt in his mind as to what we were alluding, nor did he hesitate in pronouncing "cookie" when desire arose. This meant that he *could* learn to understand and speak, given time and expert help. I wondered what this therapy would consist of. I had a vague image of Evan, his senses miraculously sharpened by medication, spending most of each day in a hospital-like atmosphere while therapists worked expertly with him in their quest for the "key." What highly skilled techniques would they use? I was impatient to get him started on his therapeutic program, for with each passing day I became more conscious that valuable time was being wasted.

I realized that in my usual preoccupied manner of going about our daily routine I was missing opportunities to build language understanding for Evan. I immediately established new ways. I formed the habit of providing a simple verbal commentary along with our daily activities: "We are going to *school,*" "Evan is taking a *bath,*" "*We* are eating lunch." I also began choosing very carefully the words I used to instruct him. I used only the important words and pronounced them slowly and emphatically, repeating them a couple of times. "Eat-eat-your-dinner," "Get-in, get-in-the tub." Each day I used exactly the same words at the same time, indicating by gesture what I wanted him to do. Soon I was dropping the gestures, for he quickly learned to recognize my instructions.

I searched the stores for "educational" toys and brought them home to Evan, but he was rarely interested in them. I seized upon his fondness for music and bought records of nursery rhyme songs, and played them every evening. I resolved to fill his days with words.

Don and I had decided there was a great deal of doubt as to whether Evan had any motor impairment or not. Dr. Ward had mentioned a flat-footed walk, but I remembered later that I had watched Evan as Dr. Ward had led him slowly down the long hospital corridor. Evan had been slapping his feet on the tile floor, enjoying the sound they made. This was not his natural walk at all, but Dr. Ward could not have known that. Evan's handling of his silverware and so forth was certainly very immature, but, we reasoned, we had not really made a point of insisting he do things for himself, so perhaps our laxity was at fault. In any event, motor impairment was not a severe problem, so it seemed the solution here was simply to encourage him to learn to eat properly, dress himself and to refrain from assisting him so quickly in simple matters such as unwrapping a piece of candy.

The matter of Evan's visual perception was definitely an unknown factor. How did he see things? How could we know? Certainly we noticed nothing unusual in most of his activities. I remembered, however, my continual failure to interest him in books. It was not only the words that went over his head; he was not interested in the pictures either. Now, trying again, I showed him pictures of things I knew he should be familiar with. Watching him closely, I saw no flicker of recognition in his eyes as

45

he glanced at page after page and restlessly flipped them over. I was fairly certain that a picture of a house, a tree, a boy was only an unrelated mass of colors to him. No wonder he disliked books! I now realized why he always smelled everything. His other senses were unreliable.

I had no idea how I or anyone else could help him with the visual problem. In any event, our most important problem was communication. Without it we could not help him with anything.

At night I did not allow myself to think about Evan's trouble. In the dark one is too vulnerable to pain and despair. Always an insomniac, I now conceived the trick of envisioning my mind as a long mane of hair. As taboo thoughts tried to force their way into my consciousness, I quickly "combed" them out, combing and combing until sleep came. Oddly, I have tried this trick since but it has never worked again. Only during that time when it was so vital.

About three weeks after our visit with Dr. Ward, Evan caught his finger in a sliding door and I took him to our pediatrician to be treated. The doctor had received Dr. Ward's report and gave me a summary of it. He concluded with the words "functionally retarded." The term was unfamiliar to me.

"What does that mean?" I frowned. "Does it mean mentally retarded?"

The doctor nodded. "Yes," he said, simply.

After a shocked silence, my own instincts came to the fore and I said, "I can't accept that."

What I meant was that I simply could not believe it, but the doctor apparently took my words to mean I would not face it.

Removing his glasses and carefully wiping them, he said slowly, "We all want our children to be intelligent and successful. We look upon them as an extension of ourselves . . ."

46

"It isn't that," I interrupted. "It's what they will have to go through." I felt almost pitying. I knew he had no children, was not even married. He apparently had not experienced the kind of love that transcends selfish desires, psychological clichés, a love where the feelings of the loved one are the only important thing. I had studied some psychology, but I knew from experience that one cannot take human emotion, sort it and file it under textbook titles.

"Well, yes, what they will have to go through," conceded the doctor.

"Dr. Ward said that although Evan failed the mentality test, it didn't necessarily mean anything," I argued. "Evan's comprehension was so limited he really wasn't able to be tested accurately." I didn't understand. If the psychologist had decided that Evan was mentally retarded, why had he told us he didn't know? And why use this term, *"functionally* retarded"?

"It may be years before they can get a good test," the doctor now agreed.

"I just don't think he's mentally retarded," I repeated stubbornly.

"Well," the doctor said in a confidential tone, "I don't either."

Not caring to speculate over the pediatrician's rather sudden change in attitude, I took his words at face value and, counting another ally for our team, I went home encouraged.

At last it was time for our appointment with Dr. Carson. He was very much as we had imagined him and yet he was not. He had the skill, the sureness of the born diagnostician, but he was completely lacking in the perhaps unwitting brusqueness that is sometimes characteristic of those who have attained the heights in their field. He asked us many questions about Evan, his development and behavior, and it was his questions that made me really see something for the first time. Evan had changed very little during the past year or more; he was very much as he had been at age two or less. From birth he had progressed at a normal rate, and then he almost stopped—just about the time most children are achieving some language skill. While other children were continuing to progress and learn with their new tool, communication, Evan had been left behind. I had been so close to him I hadn't seen it.

Dr. Carson examined Evan, gently, expertly. Far from being frightened as usual by medical probings, Evan lapsed into giggles. These giggling fits were usually as hard to turn off as tantrums, and I was amazed when the doctor ended it with a slight shake of his head and a finger to his lips, "No-shhh." Evan sobered cooperatively, apparently forgetting that the word "no" was always his cue to fly into a shrieking rage.

I told Dr. Carson that I became filled with confusion when asked how much speech Evan had. He could *say* just about anything, but he didn't seem to know the *meaning* of many words.

The doctor nodded understandingly. "Does he echo? Repeat what you have just said?"

"Exactly! He echoes!" The word and my recognition that this was apparently a common symptom of aphasia cleared up my muddled thinking on this point.

At the conclusion of his examination, Dr. Carson told us that his diagnosis confirmed Dr. Ward's. Evan was, in his professional opinion, neurologically handicapped; his principal symptom, aphasia. He spoke of the training, the special schooling that Evan would have to have, "and I mean years and years and years." He pronounced these words with quiet emphasis, making sure they sank in. He talked of the need for structure in the home, orderliness of house and schedule. These children needed to know what to expect to minimize their frustrations and strengthen their security. Don and I smiled. Something else we were unwittingly doing right. As Don remarked to Dr. Carson, I was something of a fanatic on orderliness and schedule. I seemed to need it to avoid frustration myself.

After satisfying himself that Don and I fully understood our situation, Dr. Carson gave us a note personally requesting additional tests: an EEG, a hearing test and a speech evaluation. He then had an assistant direct us to the different parts of the hospital where we could make these appointments. After we had done this, the assistant arranged for our second appointment with Dr. Carson. This was to be at the conclusion of all the tests, when he could summarize the findings.

After our visit with Dr. Carson, I realized that I had felt no shock, no dashed hopes. I, too, was already certain that Evan was aphasic. Dr. Carson's confirmation was but the starting point for action. The tests he had scheduled were all to be in the next two weeks, so we would be getting Evan started on therapy soon.

In the past few weeks I had become increasingly aware of some of the complexities of Evan's aphasia. The trouble was not merely that he did not understand the meaning of most words, but much more. He had no conversational concepts. He did not know what a question was, or an answer; he did not really have any idea of the way

50

in which language is used. I had realized, too, that he understood even less than I had thought. For example, when I said, "Sit down at the table," he did so; but I now found that no single word in this phrase meant anything to him. I had so often uttered these exact words as I helped him to his place that the entire sound, "sitdown-atthetable," was simply a stimulus for this specific action.

Nor did he even use his one complete phrase, "Want some (apple, cookie, water)" in a really meaningful way. He had no understanding that the word "want" expressed a desire. He was hopefully repeating the same sound that always accompanied an offering—"want-some?"

I now also understood why Evan's handicap portended so much tragedy. Not to comprehend language is to be cut off from the source of most knowledge. Even certain things that might be learned by experiencing them can be lost through lack of an explanation accompanying the experience. The idea of Christmas as a holiday or celebration might pass over the aphasic child completely. The different manifestations—Santa Claus, presents, tree, turkey—may seem quite unrelated to him. Thus, unable to understand our world, he cannot really be a part of it.

Evan lagged not only in language itself. His lack of verbal understanding had already prevented him from learning a thousand things other small children knew. Three-year-olds are normally already driving their parents to distraction with "why" questions. Their lively curiosities are at work, piling up knowledge of the world around them, seeking explanations of all they do not understand. Evan could not ask "Why?" He had no concept of the word. The knowledge that he "picked up" was strictly limited to his own direct experiences. There were no explanations to clarify things for him or to give him knowledge of the world outside his own sphere.

51

It occurred to me that his thought processes themselves must be crippled by his lack of language. How much of our thinking is done with words? I experimented, trying to think without using mental speech, and I found it confusing and actually disorienting. I knew this could not be an accurate impression of Evan's thinking. I had to make an effort to deny myself this mental aid; Evan was unaware of it. Still, I realized that the more complex the thought, the more I relied upon language.

Yes, it was easy to see how aphasia could cause retardation. It was time to think of what I could not before—the danger of Evan being relegated to the dim world of the retarded. First of all, I was certain that Evan had above average intelligence. There was no way of proving it. I might have to go on faith for years, and I would have to hold to this faith no matter what, unless positively proven otherwise. I had decided that, for reasons of his own, our pediatrician had deliberately misled me upon the definition of "*functionally* retarded." Dr. Ward had not pulled his punches. I could not believe that he would have told us he did not know whether or not Evan had a normal inner potential, and put it on record that he had not. No, it did not take a great deal of analyzing to deduce that the term merely meant that Evan's *functioning* was not at a normal level. The psychologist had told us that, anyway. Surely, our pediatrician had not spoken out of ignorance. More likely, he thought that Evan's case was hopeless and that I might as well learn to accept retardation as a fact from the start. As for his rather abrupt change of attitude at the conclusion of our visit, he was probably simply humoring a stubborn mama who was not yet ready to face the inevitable. Well, he was right about my stubbornness; I had no intention of giving up before we had even begun.

Assuming, then, that the intellectual potential was present, there had to be a way of getting to it. The problem was to find the way, but find it we would. Had Dr. Ward said "often" these children grew to be retarded, or had he said "usually"? I could not remember. I only knew that he had not said "always." If the odds were a million to one, then Evan would make it. We would make sure of it, find the very best for him, no matter what it took. If one was determined enough, one could do anything. Annie Sullivan had proven that with Helen Keller. We could not afford to lose any more time. We had to begin the search for that "key" Dr. Ward had spoken of.

Evan's speech evaluation was our first important step in this search. The evaluation was to be conducted at a center where children received therapy for language disorders, where, perhaps, Evan would be going. The center was brand-new and just opening its doors under the direction of a Sister Elizabeth. Our appointment was for nine o'clock in the morning.

Being one of those people who has all the directional instincts of a wind-up doll, I drove around for quite a while before noticing that a modest little house bore the name of the speech center. In the reception room Evan curiously examined the toys that had been thoughtfully placed there, and I looked at my surroundings with interest, wondering how much time I might be spending in them. Two children, apparently there for therapy, seemed no different from any children, and their mothers, preoccupied with magazines, seemed as casual as if on a routine trip to the dentist. Were these children like Evan? If so, would I ever get used to the idea as these mothers seemed to have done?

Soon, a tiny nun in a modified habit stepped briskly into the room. Her eyes found Evan at once, and she said, "Evan-will-you-come-with-me-please?" She pronounced each word separately and distinctly, and although I knew that his name was the only word he understood, Evan followed her as if she were the pied piper.

Sister Elizabeth cheerfully motioned for me to come also, and feeling somehow large and ungainly at five-foot-three, I too joined the procession. Inside her office, the Sister and Evan sat at a small table on which was placed a puzzle. I had never seen a puzzle like it before. Instead of being a fragmented picture or object, each piece was an entire object itself. There was a ball, a house, a doll; and each piece had a small knob for easy handling.

Taking one piece at a time, Sister Elizabeth asked Evan, "What is this? Tell me."

Eager to cooperate, for he obviously had felt an immediate rapport with the Sister, Evan echoed her words "tell me." He wanted very much to do whatever it was she was asking, but he just could not understand her simple phrases. When he was unable to answer, she would say the proper word. "Ball," she told him, and he repeated "ball." But when she then picked up a house, he again said "ball." Several times he interjected "Evan."

"He is trying very hard but he obviously does not understand. He knows I want him to speak. You see, someone has taught him his name, and he is saying it, hoping to please me. My, what a beautiful child," continued the Sister. "His features are just exquisite! And those eyes are full of intelligence. Yes, you can see that he has a very bright mind."

At last someone was speaking my language! Ten minutes and she already saw Evan as we did, or rather, I thought, as he was. This was where Evan belonged. There was no doubt in my mind.

"I don't believe he really sees those puzzle pieces as what they represent, Sister," I said. "I mean, he would probably say 'ball' if you showed him a real one, but he doesn't see that piece as a ball. It's only a piece of wood to him."

"Yes, I'm quite sure you're right," the Sister nodded. "I don't believe he is interpreting what he sees. You certainly have accepted him, Mrs. Cameron," she remarked, studying Evan.

Her comment rather startled me. The idea of not accepting our dearly loved little boy was unthinkable. Later, I would recall this remark when I caught an unwelcome glimpse of the heartbreaking predicaments some of these children were in.

Sister Elizabeth asked me more questions. Did Evan insist that certain things always be done in exactly the same way? Wasn't the result rather catastrophic if they were not? She seemed to know him as well as I did.

"I see that he has not had his hearing tested yet, but I'm quite sure they won't find a problem there," Sister Elizabeth went on. She knocked on the wall and Evan, now playing in the center of the room with his back toward us, turned sharply to see where the noise had come from.

"I believe he has classic aphasia. That is, his aphasia is both receptive and expressive. It's a little unusual. More often a child will have just one problem. I would like to start him in therapy, if you agree. In the beginning it will be diagnostic therapy to determine just how much he can understand and say."

I was nodding enthusiastically, and she picked up the telephone. "I'll see if I can contact Dr. Carson now."

Oh, she was marvelous! She was no more willing to waste any time than I was.

"Dr. Carson is out of his office just now but he will return my call when he comes back," Sister Elizabeth told me, replacing the receiver and rising from her desk. "When I talk to him I will tell him what I think and what I would like to do. Then I will let you know. I'm sure he'll agree."

Our interview was at an end. Thanking the Sister, I

departed with Evan, feeling as if our battle was already half won. This little nun would be no more willing than I to accept anything less than Evan's complete fulfillment of his potential. I was as sure of her as I was of myself.

A few hours later I received a call from the speech center. Evan had been scheduled for therapy on Mondays and Fridays, would that be all right? He could start this Friday. But Evan had his hearing test on that day so we arranged for him to begin therapy the next Monday. I was rather surprised that he was to have therapy only twice a week and for only half an hour at a time. Whatever it was they did must be very effective.

What a relief to have Evan finally getting professional help! I was grateful for the expediency with which his admission was handled but I could not have known how truly fortunate we were. I was ignorant of the shortage of such clinics, and the long waiting lists they usually had. We had come at the magic moment. This speech center was just getting started; a few months more and we would have been placed on their own growing waiting list.

And so we began the thirty-mile round trips to the center which were to become so much a part of our lives. Evan's therapist was a young woman, and while I waited in the reception room, she worked with him for thirty minutes twice a week.

It was time for us to go back and see Dr. Carson again. Evan had had all his tests now and Dr. Carson was to give us a final summary of the results. He had, of course, already given us his own initial diagnosis, and with the exception of the EEG, we knew the results of the tests. Although it was difficult to give Evan a conventional hearing test because of his lack of verbal comprehension, the audiologist had concluded that his hearing was normal. The Sister, of course, had told me her opinion during our interview. Thus, we were not now expecting to hear anything that would change what we already knew of Evan's condition, particularly since Dr. Carson had given his okay for Evan to begin therapy.

Evan was not to come along on this visit, and I suggested to Don that since we already knew the facts, it was not really necessary that he take more time off from work. The truth was, I wanted to ask Dr. Carson for the kind of personal (if well-educated) opinions that physicians are often reluctant to give in such cases, and I was afraid that the presence of more than one of us might make this difficult. In short, I was planning to put the doctor on the spot.

I was struck once more by the gracious kindness of this man as he greeted me. He wasted no time in banalities, however, but went immediately to the test results. The EEG had showed some brain damage, "rather severe in this area," Dr. Carson said, as he gestured toward the top left side of his head, "which is pretty much what we would expect, considering the symptoms." All of the tests served to reinforce Dr. Ward's original diagnosis: neurologically handicapped, specifically aphasic.

"Functionally retarded does not necessarily mean mentally retarded, does it, Dr. Carson?" I asked. I wanted to settle that question, once and for all.

"No, no, it means that the child is simply lagging in performance. He may or may not have normal intelligence," the physician answered.

"Do you think that Evan is mentally retarded, Doctor?" I had to know what he thought even if it was something I could not accept.

"Well, there is no way of determining that right now," Dr. Carson began. "Sometimes the damage is limited to certain brain functions, or it may be more extensive and affect the mentality. My personal opinion is that Evan is probably not mentally retarded, but there is no way to tell for sure."

His answer was more than I had dared hope for. I had been afraid that even if I succeeded in getting his opinion it would not be what I wanted to hear. Nothing could shake my faith now!

"What about his future?" I asked. "What kind of a life can we expect for Evan when he grows up?"

"We have no way of predicting. We really don't like to even venture a guess, because we simply can't know," said the doctor kindly.

"Yes, I know you can't know and I know you hate to conjecture," I persisted, "but please, just tell me this: What usually happens to children like Evan? Do they grow up to be retarded?"

"Well, again, we don't even like to think in general terms about them because each is an individual and can develop in an individual way——"

"But . . ." I began to interrupt. The doctor silenced me with a kind nod and went on.

"Children who are not too severely damaged usually are able to learn and grow up fairly normally, but those who have sustained more severe damage—well, usually they are not able to overcome it. However, rather than thinking to the years ahead, it is important to learn to take just a day at a time, and concentrate on that."

"Yes," I nodded, "I know and I'm not going to worry about the future. I feel so optimistic, I just *know* that Evan is going to make it."

It was true. I knew that Evan belonged to that more severely damaged group that usually did not "make it," and I had no clear idea of how we would make him one of the exceptions. But I knew that, whatever it took, we would. Obviously, the usual treatment was not enough for children like Evan. We would get him more. I was grateful to Dr. Carson for answering me so candidly, and he was obviously pleased with my anything but despairing reaction to his words as he smiled encouragingly at me.

58

"Well, that's wonderful. That's the way to feel." He looked again at the paper in front of him. "Is Evan hyper- active?" he asked.

"Yes," I nodded. I had been waiting for this to come up. Now Dr. Carson would be prescribing one of the drugs Dr. Ward had told us of. I was hoping against hope that medication would provide at least part of the answer to our problem. If the proper nerves could be stimulated so that Evan could concentrate and learn . . .

Dr. Carson jotted down a prescription for a drug com- monly used with hyperactive children.

Let this be the one, I prayed, as he handed me the slip of paper.

"Now, one more thing," said Dr. Carson. "Evan should have some sort of supervised play with other children."

"He has been going to nursery school for almost a year now," I said, pleased that yet another of Evan's needs was already being met.

"Oh, fine, that's very good." Dr. Carson smiled again. Something in his manner radiated encouragement. He showed me out, telling me that when Evan reached school age, he should be evaluated again. If we had any problems or questions in the meantime, we should feel welcome to call upon him.

So it was over. All the tests had been given, the results were in, the diagnosis made. It was serious, as serious as it could be, and the prognosis was, to say the least, uncertain. Yet, aside from the two half-hour therapy sessions per week, Evan's life was to go on very much as before. Realizing this, I suddenly felt letdown. I really didn't know what I had expected, but certainly not life as before.

A monumental battle had to be fought to avert a potential tragedy, and I felt that we were very alone. Normally when someone is dangerously ill or injured, physicians are in constant attendance. Now there were no doctors about. There was nothing they could do.

Adding to my frustration, Evan's medication had not been successful. It had overstimulated him and he had gone without sleep for thirty-six hours. A second drug prescribed by the pediatrician had been almost equally disastrous. I made an appointment with him. Ostensibly my purpose was to report on the medication and to discuss the report from Dr. Carson, which our pediatrician should have received. Actually, I was more impelled by the uneasy feeling that a doctor should be observing Evan.

The pediatrician was kind and obviously interested in Evan's case, but he had nothing to add to the report. It was apparent, he said, that Evan was one of those who simply did not respond to the usual medications. After some searching in a heavy book, he decided to put Evan on a simple mild tranquilizer. Although this should calm him, it would not have the effect we had hoped for from the stimulants. Another door was to be closed to us. The pediatrician said that he would like to see Evan every three months instead of the usual six. Then, since there was really nothing more to do or to say, our interview drew to a close.

A checkup four times a year—no, there were no answers here!

All right, I'll find them myself, I thought, as I drove home. I was suddenly angry at a world that could send men into space, could do vital organ transplants, could talk matter-of-factly of creating life in a test tube, but could do so little to assure my little boy the kind of future that was his birthright.

What would I get for Evan if I could, I asked myself, as I tossed sleeplessly in bed that night.

The world's greatest expert on aphasia to constantly attend and devote himself exclusively to Evan was the obvious if unrealistic answer. But I was not fantasizing, I was charting our course. Yes, that would be the ultimate. That "very best" we were looking for. This was what Evan must have. Obviously, we could not obtain such services from this "greatest aphasia expert," whoever he might be, so the only alternative was for me to become such a person. Yes, I would make myself into an expert, not on aphasia itself but on *Evan's* aphasia—the world's greatest expert on Evan himself.

I had always felt that anyone could do anything if he really wanted to enough and tried hard enough, and my confidence did not waver now. People almost never used their maximum powers. I must call on mine now, stretch my intelligence to its very limit. I must study Evan, search for ways of teaching him to communicate, analyze carefully the methods that were most effective. I must see that information was constantly flowing to his brain; never allow it to be cut off. I would be the link between him and the world until he learned to understand. I had a precedent to guide me—Annie Sullivan. She had obtained her goal primarily through determination. I, too, possessed that weapon. Annie had worked her miracle on Helen Keller. I would work mine on Evan.

I began the next morning. I must see that there were

no wasted hours in Evan's day, that some sort of educational process was constantly taking place. So it is with normal children. They are continually absorbing information and expanding their understanding in a remarkable process of which even the most observant parent is rarely aware.

Some of Evan's time was already satisfactorily employed. The three mornings a week at nursery school were of vital importance. Being with other children and participating in constructive activities with them was, perhaps, the most important thing he did. It went without saying that the two half-hour therapy sessions were valuable. My only regret here was that so little time was involved in this endeavor.

With nursery school and therapy, Evan was involved in some positive activity five mornings a week. This still left a great deal of unoccupied time, and Evan did not know how to occupy his time. He did not know how to play as other children did. Most children play by pretending, but Evan did not know how to pretend. Whatever potential imagination he might have was as yet unborn, unfertilized by a word, an idea. So Evan spent his hours at home following me around from room to room watching me perform my hardly entertaining tasks. These hours were what I concentrated on now; I *must* find a way to make this time productive.

I had already begun the practice of providing a brief explanation with our various daily activities—"We are going to *school,* ""Mama is *cooking*"—and carefully wording my instructions to him in the same way every day: "Get in the tub," "Eat your lunch." Although I felt that Evan was gaining some comprehension, particularly of the instructions, I did not delude myself that he was learning to understand the meaning of the separate words in these phrases. It was a beginning, nothing more.

63

I had also started routinely pointing to objects and naming them for him, but so far I had noticed no dramatic results. I now decided to be more selective and methodical. With each separate activity—eating, for instance—I would name just one object several times and repeat this procedure every time we engaged in this activity. Only when I was sure he knew the name for one object would I go on to another. Thus, at mealtime I started with "spoon." At bathtime it was "towel." While dressing, our lesson was "shoes." And so forth.

Since Evan was echolalic and his instinctive reaction was to repeat what was said to him, it was easy to get him to say the words. I was careful to say only the name of the object; never "this is a spoon," for he would repeat my words verbatim, assuming the object's name was "thisisaspoon." After several repetitions I would hold the spoon—or whatever object we were working on—in front of him and say "Evan?" rather sharply and questioningly. He understood that I wanted him to say the proper word. Sometimes, to get across what I wanted, it helped to give the object an emphatic shake in front of his face or grasp his shoulder to command his attention. This one-object-at-a-time-per-activity method worked well, and he was usually ready to go on to another object in two or three days. Then I might hold the spoon before him and when he had correctly identified it as a "spoon," I would then take the fork and proceed in the same manner. It took Evan little time to understand what we were doing, and he seemed eager to play our game. He was learning several new words at a time, but they were separated in his mind by the specific activity each was associated with. Thus, he did not confuse them. My earlier method of naming several things at once—"spoon, knife, fork, plate, napkin"—had probably not only confused him but made the task seem too great to attempt.

I was playing the nursery song records for Evan for

64

an hour each evening. He immensely enjoyed these sessions, listened closely to the songs and learned rather quickly to sing them. Although this activity did nothing to answer his most desperate need, comprehension, he was at least engaged in *learning,* and in learning something that might bring him a small step closer to other children. I also attempted to interest him in looking at books, working puzzles and other normal childish pleasures, but with very limited success. No time was passing, then, without some effort being made: school, therapy, vocabulary building, a guided program of normal play.

Evan's emotional home situation was already apparently almost ideal, I reflected with satisfaction. We had always "sort of spoiled him," which Dr. Ward had said was recommended treatment. Certainly no child had ever been more loved. As his sisters were so much older than he, there was a notable absence of the rivalry and resentment that often complicate sibling relationships.

Our home life was well ordered. I had always kept my rooms tidy for my own satisfaction; there was no visual confusion. We followed a fairly set routine that contributed to Evan's sense of security. I realized now why this sameness of routine was so important. He had learned to cope with his world as best he could with his impaired senses, and even minor changes shook his rather precarious self-confidence. He was much as a blind person who expects the furniture in his home to be arranged in a certain way. If he stumbles over a chair that has been moved to a new location, his entire self-assurance is undermined.

It would seem that the maximum effort was being made. Yet I knew that it was not enough.

Nursery school, for all its advantages, did little to assist Evan in learning to communicate. He hardly spoke in school at all, they told me, and he gave little evidence of even attempting to listen to teachers or children.

I knew now that the speech therapy could not produce

the kind of miracle so urgently needed. I had discovered that I could observe Evan's therapy sessions by means of a two-way mirror installed in the door of the room. The therapist worked with Evan by using various instructive toys: puzzles such as Sister Elizabeth had used in her evaluation, different colored plastic rings, variously shaped blocks and so forth. I saw that her intentions were to stimulate Evan's speech and at the same time instruct him in basic concepts through this play.

The trouble was that Evan was not cooperating. He refused to say things I knew he could, and would not attempt many of the simple maneuvers I knew he was capable of. He seemed to spend a great deal of the precious time on the floor deliberately ignoring the therapist or even tantrumming. This was going to take time. Too much time!

The same was true of what we were doing at home. Evan was definitely making steady progress in our vocabulary-building program, but even so it would be years, if ever, before this method would produce enough comprehension to convey a thought, an idea. Of what use were the words "spoon," "towel," "dress," "car," when I wanted to tell my child about people, the world, the universe?

The enemy was time—or, rather, the lack of it. Success, if it came, would be too late. Surely Evan was already realizing that he was different from the other children at school. As that fact became more and more obvious to him, he would become so accustomed to the idea that he compared unfavorably with his peers that his poor self-image would be permanent. No, even if we were to establish some meaningful communication in just a few years, Evan would already be convinced of his own incompetence. He would have given up trying to bridge the ever-widening gap between himself and others his age. I envisioned Evan's intellect becoming dulled from lack of stimulation, as a muscle withers from want of exercise.

I had to do more—but what?

Evan had never napped, at least not since he was an infant, but I always put him in his room by himself for a couple of hours after lunch. This was the only time that he ever played with his toys, and although he did not play with them in the normal way, I felt that learning to amuse himself was an important part of his development. Of course, having some time to myself was not unwelcome either! It now occurred to me that some of this time might be turned to a greater profit. An hour or so of solitary play should be sufficient.

One afternoon when Evan had been in his room for about half an hour, I entered, closing the door behind me so he would not think his rest period was over. I had absolutely no plan in mind, so sitting down on the floor with him, I looked around for an idea. I pointed to a few toys and pronounced their names. Evan, understanding this game well by now, obediently repeated after me. That took all of two minutes or so, and I again searched my mind for inspiration. Just naming toy after toy would not accomplish anything. I had already discovered that he could not learn several words at one time without confusing them.

Taking one of his blocks, I emphatically said, "block!" I pointed to his toy train and said, "Train." I then lifted the block onto the little flatcar and said, "Put the block on the train." I repeated the entire procedure four or five times, and then tried to get Evan to "put the block on the train" when I spoke. He echoed my phrase but did not seem to understand that the words were intended to prompt the action. I tried again—this time with my hand upon his, helping him perform the act. Still no luck. I tried to project my idea with different objects. We put the block on the *bus,* we put the *key* on the train. No

67

response. He simply did not understand. After a time I left, discouraged.

I tried again the next day and the next. Evan learned to name a couple of toys he had not been able to before, but as for "putting the block on the train," I had no more success than I had the first day.

We were really getting nowhere, I pondered. Even if we were to go on until he could name every toy in his room, we would not really be accomplishing anything momentous. I must find a way to convey *ideas* to him.

I needed a whole new approach. I had to reorganize my thinking, analyze what I wanted to do. So I wanted to "convey ideas" to Evan, did I? Laudable, I told myself sarcastically, but appallingly vague. What ideas? If I were going to get anywhere, I'd better begin with a clearer definition. *Ideas* was too hazy; *concepts* was a more accurate term. Yes, that gave me a defined goal. I would teach Evan concepts—but where to begin? Obviously, at the beginning. What was the first concept a child learned? My thinking clouded again at the unanswerable question. All right then, what was the first concept a child was expected to know?

Colors and shapes! In kindergarten Cindy and Wendy had had to be able to identify colors and shapes!

I now had something definite to work with. Evan had some plastic blocks in various shapes and colors. They were red, blue, yellow, green, orange and purple, and there was a square, a round, a triangular block in each color. These would be perfect for teaching purposes.

The night after my mental regrouping, I lay awake carefully detailing the first step in my teaching plan. The next afternoon I went into Evan's room and sat down on the floor with him just as I had been doing. For several minutes we played with the blocks and the train. Then, as if I had suddenly had a delightful inspiration, I said, "Oh, *Evan!* I have an idea!" I always spoke to him as if he could understand me; and he, of course, did get general impressions from my tone.

I led him to the little table and chairs against one wall. Seating him at one end of the table, I scooped up the pile of plastic blocks which I had been surreptitiously gathering and sat down at the opposite end. I took a round block and, rolling it down the table to him, exclaimed "rrrrrround!" Evan squealed with glee, and I laughed too as if at the game. We were having fun! I rolled the remaining round blocks to him one at a time, each time pronouncing "rrrrrround!" Then I took the square blocks and gave each a gentle toss so that it landed flat in front of Evan. "Square," I said, trying to made the word sound concise. I slid each triangle to him on one side; the length of the word "triangle" rather conveniently fit this motion. With each roll, toss or slide, I gave an ecstatic giggle, and Evan became so overcome with laughter he could hardly remain on his chair. Hardly an ideal teaching atmosphere, but the important thing now was to make him think we were playing a game. I went through the entire procedure once more with Evan. Then, going back to the floor, we played with other toys for a few minutes before I left.

On the second day I proceeded in the same way, but this time I would "forget" to call the third or fourth "round," "square" or "triangle" by name as I propelled it to him. He began to unconsciously supply the proper word himself. On the third afternoon, I changed my presentation slightly. Instead of giving Evan all the "rounds" at one time, then the "squares," then the "triangles," I grouped the blocks according to color. Taking the red group, I gave him the square, then the round, then the triangle, and so on with the remaining color groups. Always, however, I propelled the blocks to him in the same manner as before.

After several days I held up each block before sending

69

it down the table and asked, "What's this?" Evan did not understand my words but he knew by my tone and gestures that I was asking him to verbally identify the object. Surprisingly, for I would have bet on the "rrrround," the triangle was the first shape he correctly named. The round and the square followed within two or three days.

I was beginning to discover how this type of teaching could indirectly build speech. Evan was not only learning to recognize shapes, he was learning the meaning of the verbal question "What's this?" He now intuitively understood by my manner that I was asking for identification; through constant repetition and association he would eventually understand the words by themselves.

Soon Evan was naming every single block correctly. I mixed them up, presented them this way and that. It made no difference; I failed to catch him up.

There was no mistake about it. Evan had learned to verbally identify shapes. He possessed concept! He *could* learn! I *could* teach him!

We were on our way!

did not know it but Evan and I had embarked upon the first, and by far the most important, phase of a definitive educational program. I certainly did not think of what I was doing in such presumptuous terms as "program," "system" or "method." I was groping along in the dark with no idea of where the next step would lead us. I had decided that I would simply teach Evan all that he was capable of learning. If we came to something which I felt he truly could not learn, we would quickly back away from it and go on to something else.

In looking back, with the aid of a brief diary, I can see that what we did assumes the form of a rather defined system. At the time, however, I hardly noticed that our program went through definite stages, and I was quite unaware of the overall significance of each stage. During the first six months we went through two distinct sub-phases, which together comprised the most critical period of Evan's education. The whole of his subsequent education depended upon these six months.

Now, however, we had only begun our sessions in the little room with the small table and chairs. Evan had learned his shapes. Now for his colors.

Confidently, I began. I propelled the blocks to him in the usual manner, but now I exclaimed, "*Red* square!" "*Purple* square!" "*Green* square!" and so on. Evan did say the word for the shape with me but he omitted the color word. I presented the blocks in color groups: "*red* square, *red* round, *red* triangle!" No response. No flicker of interest in the color aspect of the blocks. I continued these exercises with him day after day, but when I held up a block and inquired, "What's this?" he identified only the shape, never the color. Boredom was not the problem, for he still enjoyed the game (perseveration can have its advantages). Why wasn't he catching on?

Since learning colors was evidently going to take some time, I decided to work on something else as well. What would be good, I wondered, as I searched through Evan's toys for an idea. My eyes fell on some little plastic animals that had come with a toy zoo train. Every child knew most of his animals—usually from picture books. Evan could learn them too from these three-dimensional replicas.

Positioned at the little table in our customary manner, I took the little animals and one by one maneuvered them down the table. I attempted to give each a distinguishing gait to make the game interesting. "Elephant!" I exclaimed, and made the animal plod heavily down the table, muttering "lumber, lumber, lumber." I endowed the horse with a brisk trot, and after announcing "Horse!" I accompanied its quick trip down the table with the words "gallop, gallop, gallop." Evan shrieked with laughter when we played this game, and within a very short time could name all of the animals. My standard "what's this" as I held up an object was always understood now.

I rather wished that I had used only the individual names of the animals and omitted the words that described their gaits, for this confused Evan a bit at first. When I asked him what the elephant was, he invariably answered "lumber-lumber," and it took a little extra time to straighten him out on this.

We were still going through our colored block routine every day but had made no progress at all on colors. He was repeating his shapes daily, however, and I felt this was important. He had learned his shapes. There was no doubt about that, but I wanted to make sure he forgot nothing. More than that, really, I had the idea of *drilling in*, by countless repetitions, the things that I was teaching him. I wanted the concepts, the words, to become deeply ingrained upon his mind so that they actually became a part of him. I theorized that eventually, when he saw a square for instance, there would be no groping or even hesitation in identifying it. The knowledge would be *there.*

The block and animal exercises together took little more than ten minutes, and Evan's interest did not wane at all by the end of this time. We could easily be accomplishing more, I realized. I decided to expand our "curriculum." Evan had proven that he could learn in a simulated academic manner, that is, methodical memorization. Why not give him English lessons in the way foreign languages are taught in school? I had been rather good in French, but I doubted seriously that I could ever have learned it by living among French people and assimilating the language. I had learned methodically, by studying and memorizing carefully planned lessons. I would include vocabulary instruction in our daily sessions. I remembered my first French classes very well. We had begun by learning the names for every object in our classroom—book, pencil, window, and so on. Evan and I would start our English lessons the same way.

The day following my inspiration, Evan and I went through our shape-color and animal exercises as usual. Then, still seated at the table, I gave the wall a good whack. "Wall," I said. I picked up Evan's hand and pressed the palm to the wall. "Wall," I repeated until Evan echoed the word. I bent and tapped the carpet. "Floor!" I reached for Evan's hand and put it down on the red rug. "Floor." Evan obligingly repeated "floor." We said the word several times. We followed the same procedure with the picture above his table. Then we touched and named all three things again. Three words—that was enough for the first lesson, I decided.

The next day I thumped the wall and queried, "What's this?" When Evan did not respond, I repeated "What's this?" and then supplied the answer myself, *"Wall."*

(Thump.) "What's this? Wall." (Another thump.) When I came to "floor," Evan knew that one, but I had to supply the word for the picture. I had him repeat all three words two or three times apiece. The following day Evan knew both "wall" and "floor," and I added "table" and "chair" to our memorization list. We continued in this fashion day after day, always having Evan recite—while touching the objects—his known vocabulary, and making sure that there were never more than two or three unknown words on the growing list.

So absorbed was I in planning and executing our word-building system that it was not until some three weeks later that jubilant realization suddenly dawned upon me. It was working. The system was working! Evan was running and clambering about the room, touching and naming the bed, the window, the chest and so forth. In a relatively short period of time, he had acquired a confident mastery of the names for most of the important objects in his room. As he had caught onto the idea of what we were doing, he had become more eager to learn, and now was learning more quickly. He was *proud* of his accomplishments.

Proud, and something else too. What was that something, I asked myself, studying his happy and expectant face as he waited for me to demonstrate the new noun for the day. A sort of relief? Yes! The relief of a person who discovers an unlocked window when the door has been nailed shut. I was struck by the sudden thought that he had never given evidence of a desire to know the names of these objects. Perhaps he had not known these things had names, or perhaps he had known but assumed that a knowledge of them was not within his ability. Whichever, his ardent enthusiasm showed me that an important breakthrough had been made in his attitude and understanding.

The quiet, secluded atmosphere of his room and the

controlled routine of the sessions themselves were also increasing Evan's learning ability. He became conditioned to the idea that, during this period, he learned and recited, and he began to focus his mind completely upon this effort. Within these sessions he was possessed with an astonishing receptivity—much greater than that of the average child. Yet, outside of these lessons, his sensory hyperactivity (dysynchronization) was so great, he was not one-tenth as receptive as a normal child. I had read that some experts believe that children are at their most educable during the early preschool years and, judging from Evan's amazing performance, I could only agree.

During the first couple of months of lessons I would allow Evan to get up and run about the room for a minute or so between activities. As I busied myself putting away and taking out the particular toys I used for different exercises, I lost his intense concentration and hyperactivity overcame him. When I was prepared for the next exercise, I simply said, "Okay! Sit down." Evan seated himself once more and refocused his attention without difficulty. After a while he ceased to feel the need for these breaks and discontinued them of his own volition.

The pseudo-classroom routine was also helping me. I was beginning to organize my ideas as to what to teach him and when and how. We now had two periods in our academic agenda: *concept period* and *vocabulary period*. The two categories obviously overlapped, and I defined them from the point of teaching practicality. Anything that could not be readily pointed out or demonstrated would be included in concept period. For instance, "big and little" and "out and in" were verbal concepts that had to be demonstrated in several different ways before Evan could understand their meanings. Conversely, some words that involved concepts—such as the action verbs "walk," "run," "jump," etc.—could easily be demonstrated at once and taught during vocabulary period.

I began teaching Evan his verbs outside our classroom during trips to and from school and the speech center. I was training myself to find ways of turning unproductive time into learning experiences for Evan, just as an efficient housewife devises ways of making overlooked corners of her home functional. Proceeding from the car to our destination at our usual pace, I suddenly tugged at Evan's arm and broke into a run. "Run!" I called, throwing excitement into my voice. After five or six steps, I slowed abruptly and walked with exaggerated slowness. "Walk," I enunciated soberly, dragging the word out.

As was to be expected, Evan learned the term for the more exciting action first and was soon exhorting me to "wun!" as he pulled at my hand. It took more prodding to get him to pronounce the word "walk." For the first time I was asking him to identify an action rather than a tangible object, so I was laying a new communicative pathway. After our run I walked with snail-like slowness, then used the words he associated with identification: "What's this?" These words, together with instinctive gestures—pointing to my feet, giving his arm a slight shake to get his attention focused on my message—soon produced the desired response. After a while I was able to drop the "What's this?" and say simply, "What am I *doing?*" Evan was not only learning verbs, he had learned to understand another question!

When he had added "jump" to his vocabulary, I began to put on daily performances before lunch, while the inevitable hot dog cooked. Adding new verbs one at a time, I "ran," I "walked," I "jumped," I "sat," I "stood," I "knelt," I "crawled"; all the time calling "Evan! What am I doing?" It is fortunate that no one ever happened to glance through our kitchen window, or I probably

76

would have been carried off by the appropriate keepers long ago.

Once Evan had learned to identify most of these common actions, I added "verb recitation" to the end of our vocabulary period. Every day he identified the different movements and poses as we did them together. The action itself was to be the hammer that pounded the word into his mind, just as the act of touching an object impressed its name upon his brain.

Vocabulary study was an unqualified success, but concepts! Would Evan *never* learn those colors?

had never for a moment experienced the frustrated feeling that my role as a housewife and mother was an inferior one. Indeed I had often thought, as I looked at my three children, that I was surely as important as anyone in the world. Entrusted to guide and to a great extent mold the characters of these small human beings, I held a portion of the future in my hands. The very fact that so much of my time was spent at physical tasks, requiring little or no mental activity, was a distinct advantage, for my mind was free to analyze problems, to talk with my children or just to plan creative projects. How glad I was now that I could be at home with Evan, creating the most beneficial atmosphere possible, making sure that no opportunity for learning was missed. Wherever would I have found a person to perform such a service for me, I wondered. The primary requisites for the task were an all-pervasive love and a never-absent consciousness of the crucial importance of each word, each moment. Anything less than a total and constant commitment would have been insufficient.

I had as much time for the girls as before. Actually, I may have given them more, for I made a conscious effort to see that they did not feel deprived. They were now ten and eleven and, of course, in school the greater part of the day. I often wondered how I would have managed Evan's all-important daily sessions if the girls had also been preschoolers. It would have been harder, I decided, but possible. When the girls were young they, too, had a post-lunch stay-in-your-room-quietly period and also an afternoon storyhour, during which I introduced them to the exciting world of books. I probably would have given Evan his lesson during the girls' quiet hour and read to the girls during Evan's rest period, thereby assuring all of a special time with me.

79

Possibly the most common problem parents have with the siblings of a hyperactive child is not time but the difference in discipline. Because a hyperactive child is easily upset and may tantrum at the drop of a hat, discipline must be saved for very important things. Otherwise all progress will be lost in a sea of hysteria.

Cindy and Wendy were generally understanding about their little brother's plight, but occasionally they were moved to remind me that Evan "got by" with certain things they did not at his age. My only solution was to explain the reasons for the discipline gap as fully as I could, to give them a better understanding of it. I never worried that having a handicapped brother might have a detrimental effect on the girls, for I felt that if they could not learn to hold out a helping hand to one who needed it, I would have failed miserably with them.

As I went about my business of creating and maintaining a home, my mind was engaged in trying to anticipate obstacles Evan would meet and attempting to devise methods of hurdling them. I knew that I would not have much trouble finding ways of demonstrating the concepts of size—big and little—or position—up, down, behind, beside. But what about the concept of time? How could I ever demonstrate that? And what about *God, love, fear, life, death* and similar abstract ideas?

I evolved a plan that I was later to use in our lessons, but for the time being used outside the sessions. For want of a better term, I think of this method as "familiarization." It is actually the combination of association and repetition which I was already using in certain speech concepts—"What's this?" But in this case it is aimed at an *awareness* rather than an *understanding* of a concept. I planned, for instance, to teach Evan to repeat a short bedtime prayer using the term "God" often. I could in no way give him any idea of what "God" meant, but he would become familiar with the name. Through the

80

years, he would hear and repeat this word. Sooner or later it would start the wheels of conjecture in motion in his mind. Perhaps, the two thousandth or so time he heard it, it would occur to him that he did not understand this now very familiar term, and he would begin wondering about its meaning. He would already have certain associations with the name and perhaps he would begin making a mental effort to form some image or concept from them.

The necessity for a systematic plan to force an awareness of certain words upon a person's consciousness may seem strange to those who have had no experience with a child with severe receptive aphasia. The fact is, such a child forms the habit very early of "tuning out" all conversation or words that he does not believe he is meant to understand. He hears the rapid, unintelligible language that surrounds him as a monotonous hum. The result is that what the child incidentally picks up in the way of words or ideas is almost zero.

To get Evan to "tune in" to even that language which he could understand, I had to indicate to him that I was about to say something within his comprehension. This was usually easily done by prefacing my words to him with a rather sharp "Evan!" The sharpness of the tone was necessary to lift the name out of the "hum" and capture his attention.

I did not begin the prayers just then but began our familiarization program with daily "good mornings," "good afternoons" and "good nights," as our first step toward an awareness of time. Without even having to make an effort to learn, I reasoned, he would come to associate "morning," "afternoon" and "night" with their appropriate times of day.

Evan knew what love was but he did not know the word that symbolized it. So now, every kiss, every hug was accompanied by a carefully enunciated "I *love* you." I was

81

soon getting an echoed response to this declaration: "I *wuv* you!" Even dearer, I began to awaken to the sound of "good morging!" and I would open my eyes to the chubby little face beaming with the pleasure of knowing the appropriate salutation.

Evan looked forward to our lessons; he enjoyed the unaccustomed mental challenge. Occasionally, toward the end of the half-hour he spent in his room before our session, he would call out "Wan-some put-the-block-on-the-train?" I had ceased bothering with that fruitless activity after the first few groping afternoons in his room; I realized that Evan was not referring to the blocks and train now. "Put-the-blocks-on-the-train" was the sound that symbolized our work period together. I could see how very far off base I had been at the beginning. Evan had no foundation on which to build such a verbal idea. My attempt to convey this idea to him was about equivalent to trying to teach addition to a child with no knowledge of numbers.

Christmas was coming and relatives sent word that they wanted gift suggestions for Evan, Puzzles, I told them. Simple wooden puzzles. He had one already and I had been having him work it in the evenings while we played his records. He had become quite proficient at this one, but I found the cardboard puzzles we had too difficult. Puzzles are a valuable educational aid for neurologically handicapped children. First of all, they are exercises in visuo-motor coordination, which such children so often have trouble with. Puzzle solving also trains children to search for differences of detail and generally develops their reasoning powers.

My parents were visiting us for Thanksgiving. Together we found, in one of our large department stores, an educational toy corner that carried a wealth of suitable toys for Evan. We found not only the common type of wooden puzzles but also the kind Evan's therapist used, where each puzzle piece was an entire object rather than a fragment of one. We bought several of these and also two number-concept toys. One of the latter was a long board on which there was a series of pegs in groups of one, two, three, four or five. A rubber square with one hole in it fit over the first peg, two squares with two holes each fit over the group of two pegs, and so on up to five. The second number toy was a series of wooden puzzles. A piece bearing the number one fit a piece with one animal on it; a piece with the number two fit a piece with two houses on it; and so forth up to the number ten piece that fit a piece imprinted with ten apples.

I was thrilled to find a miniature plastic farm with animals of the same size as the plastic zoo animals Evan had already learned. Now he could learn his domestic animals too. With the tractors, fences, wheat sheaves and even a farm family, Evan could learn all of the things associated with the word "farm."

I did not wait until Christmas but gave Evan a few of the puzzles, one at a time, during our daily lessons. Our curriculum now included puzzle period in addition to concept period and vocabulary period. I did not just give him the entire puzzle as his therapist did, but gave him the board after first removing the pieces. Then I held up each piece, and only when Evan had repeated its name after me—"ball," "baby," "house"—did I give it to him to insert in its proper place. He soon learned to recognize several of the pieces as the objects they represented rather than merely hunks of wood, and I began to insist that he name them without my prompting. Evan liked this type of puzzle and was anxious to be handed the pieces to insert. Once he realized I was going to be stubborn about it, he began to name the recognized pieces at once, and to quickly learn the unknown ones.

We worked the new puzzles of the fragmented-object type in the evening during our more relaxed play period.

83

These were not as valuable as the other puzzles at this time, for I did not feel that Evan recognized the completed pictures as the objects they represented, nor did he learn any vocabulary from them. Unlike the puzzles I used in our lessons, I left these more conventional puzzles in his room, in the hope he would occasionally attempt them on his own.

Christmas was largely lost on Evan that year of 1968. I taught him to recognize and name some of the traditional manifestations—Christmas tree, Santa Claus, present, etc.—but he possessed no understanding yet of the kind of explanatory language necessary to relate these symbols to even the vaguest concepts. Still, it was a time of excitement and fun for him, as well as for the rest of the family. Since Don was a teacher he always had two weeks of vacation at Christmas time, and it had been our custom for years to celebrate the season with several day-long excursions. This year Evan particularly enjoyed our trip to Disneyland, the highlight being the traditionally beautiful and elaborate Christmas parade. Almost as exciting, and at least as important, was our trip to the mountains to play in the snow. We rented a sled and, as I worked sporadically on a snowman, Don spent the afternoon engaged in a particularly arduous labor of love. Evan did not seem to understand why, if one could slide *down* the mountain, one could not slide *up* the mountain, and the little tyrant insisted upon sitting on the sled each time his father hauled it to the top of the slope.

On Christmas morning Evan dissolved into semihysterical cries after opening only two or three presents. The unaccustomed feverish confusion was too much for the little boy who was deprived of the privilege of anticipation. After an extra dosage of his medication previously okayed by the pediatrician and a relatively calm breakfast, Evan regained his equilibrium. I put most of his new toys away and presented them to him later, one

84

at a time, during quieter periods. I gave him the more educational toys during our lessons together in order to convey the idea to him that he was to *learn* from these toys, and because his concentration was at its peak then. The toy farm was the greatest success of all, and Evan was soon learning to identify all the animals and farm equipment. I kept the farm and other special toys high on his closet shelf. I felt that if they were allowed to be kicked around on his floor, they would lose much of their interest. I was quick to get them down upon Evan's request—"Want some farm?"—but I replaced them when he had finished with them.

As Evan began to master the names of the farm animals, I moved the playing with this toy to his evening play period. It was a time-consuming activity, and our afternoon sessions were lengthening as Evan's knowledge increased. His growing vocabulary took more and more time, and we now worked with several puzzles. In addition to the color-shape blocks and the plastic animals, our concept period now included work with counting. As he had done for two years, Evan still kept a certain set of wooden blocks lined up against his bureau. Conveniently, there were ten of these blocks, and each day I took Evan's finger and, touching it to each block, counted slowly "one-two-three-" etc. I would do this three or four times. After several daily repetitions I began to drop my voice and let Evan, who had been counting with me, take the lead.

As January began, with its usual back-to-work atmosphere, I was attacked by the determination to accomplish a certain specific project. I *had* to teach Evan his colors! His complete lack of progress in this one area was a rather large fly in the proverbial ointment. Evan had shown by his progress in our other activities that he was a fairly rapid learner. What was holding him back in learning this particular concept? Certainly, grasping an aspect of an object is more difficult than learning its name, but Evan had had no trouble learning shapes. Since he already knew the shapes of these blocks, and the difference in color was the only other differential, how could he not perceive what I was trying to get across after all this time? "*Red* square, *purple* square, *yellow* square." Day after day I had gone through this routine.

"He *must* understand!" I would think sometimes. Then again I would conjecture, "Maybe not." Perhaps he was so used to my performance he was not attempting to tune in. I would have to devise other ways of getting my idea across to him.

I made six color-coordinated piles of toys on the floor along with the blocks. "*Red* square, *red* round, *red* triangle, *red* car, red . . . etc."

I tried new techniques of identifying the colors. "Get the *red* square," I commanded to no one in particular. I crawled over and got the designated object myself to demonstrate. Then I indicated that it was his turn.

"Evan! Get the *red* square!" Evan crawled over and retrieved the yellow square and handed it to me. As I watched his face, I was aware of a veiled expression in his eyes as he continually misinterpreted my directions.

He was deliberately giving me a hard time, I decided. He knew those colors. He couldn't *not* know, after all this. He obviously did not like this work with colors. He was showing me that he would learn only those things he chose to. If I was going to be able to teach him what he needed to know, I had to break through this stubbornness.

For the next two weeks I concentrated on the different color exercises, spending the bulk of our lesson period on them. My tone became harsher, then, as I struggled for control, icy. He had to understand that we would work at this until he responded accurately!

"No, no, no, no, *no!*" I fairly shouted one afternoon

86

as Evan for the umpteenth time gave me the wrong colored object. Evan burst into sobs. I stared at him, suddenly horrified at myself. He had not the vaguest idea of what I was trying to convey! Here I was driving the bewildered child to achieve something that was simply not within his grasp. Normal learning *was* beyond him! I held him close to me, kissing his face and whispering soothing sounds. When he was quite calm and happy again, I left his room and threw myself across my bed, weeping. After a time a more rational attitude asserted itself and I made an effort to think objectively. I remembered all of the reasons that had previously given me faith that Evan's intelligence was at least normal. All of these reasons were still valid. I envisioned his brightly alert blue eyes. Uneducable? Not he!

But suppose—just *suppose*—that I was wrong. Mothers could be, particularly about their progeny's intellectual abilities. If his intelligence were below normal, he would still need to learn as much as he could. He would need to be brought to his full—if limited—potential. What I was doing could not be wrong, as long as I proceeded with caution.

I would go on as I had been, teaching Evan what he could learn but keeping in mind the possibility, no matter how remote, that my instincts were in error. I must not let him even infer impatience when he failed to grasp an idea. I could hurt him terribly if he indeed lacked the necessary ability. However, the risk of hurting him was much greater if he had the intelligence I believed and I did not go on teaching him. His therapist had still not broken through to him. Our lesson period was the only information channel open to Evan. I would continue the work with colors but with a light touch; I would stop emphasizing this one thing so.

The next afternoon I formed the six piles of objects, grouped by color, into a big circle on the floor and, sitting in the center with Evan, I took his hand and touched each pile.

"Red, blue, yellow, orange, purple, green," I chanted slowly. I indicated that he was to say the colors with me.

"Come on, Evan, r-r-re-."

"Red," Evan finally said reluctantly.

"Now, Evan, b-b-." I put his hand on the blue pile.

"Blue," said Evan.

After a couple of trips around the circle, I casually scooped up the colored objects and tossed them in a drawer. "All right! That's enough of that. Let's do the animals now!"

Relieved to have colors disposed of so easily, Evan eagerly ran to get the animals.

After a few days I discarded the piles of colored objects on the floor and, seated at our table, I formed the plastic triangles into a wheel.

"Red, blue, orange, purple, yellow, green," I said, touching each block. I took Evan's finger and touched it to each triangle, naming each individual color again. After three or four times, I went on to our next activity.

After several days of working with our multicolored wheel, I experienced another sudden onslaught of frustration. That odd, masked expression on Evan's face— that was defiance, not bewilderment! There just could not be even the remotest doubt about it.

Keeping my tone casual, I said, "Okay, Evan, shall we put the blocks away?" I touched the drawer the triangles were kept in. "Do you want to *put the blocks back?* Put them in the drawer? *Finish* with the blocks?"

Evan understood the idea I was trying to get across very well and eagerly reached for the blocks to return them to their proper place.

"Uh-uh, nope!" I interjected lightly, clapping my hands over the blocks. "First, put the *red* block away."

Evan hesitated, then picked up the yellow triangle. I took it from his hand and put it back on the table. "The *red* block, Evan."

Evan seized the blue block. I extricated it from his hand and repeated, "The *red* block."

Evan began to cry. I ignored his tears and leaned back against the wall, as if preparing to settle myself for the afternoon. I studied the ring on my finger as if it suddenly fascinated me. Each time Evan reached for a wrong block, I retrieved it, saying casually, "No, dear—*red.*"

Evan was on the horns of a dilemma. He very much wanted to finish this boring activity and go on to the puzzles and games he enjoyed. Mother seemed unresponsive to any attempt at compromise. There she sat neither sympathetic nor angry, just calmly immovable.

Finally, surrender came. As if it hurt him to move, Evan slowly picked up the red triangle and deposited it in the drawer. Careful to show no surprise, nor overwhelming delight—which might be misconstrued as triumph—I applauded with casual pleasure.

"*Very* good, Evan. Now put the *yellow* block away."

With less hesitation this time, Evan returned the yellow triangle to its drawer. Again I clapped and Evan did the same. He was not pleased nor proud but trying to find a way to cope with a new experience—defeat. I carefully maintained my casual attitude, and when Evan made a mistake on two of the blocks, I corrected him gently and gave him the proper one. I did not want him to think the victory itself held any importance for me.

It did, of course. I could hardly wait to get through our other studies so that I could leave the room to privately rejoice and speculate on the significance of what had occurred. We had just experienced an important breakthrough. I knew that. First of all, I knew with certainty now that Evan was capable of deliberately feigning ignorance; before I had only strongly suspected. I could now work with him with a confidence, a sureness of my own understanding that I had not had before.

Furthermore, the value of my new insight was not confined to our lesson periods together. Evan had displayed this perplexing apparent obtuseness at other times, most notably in nursery school and at the speech center. I had lately been particularly baffled while observing Evan in therapy. A couple of the puzzles his therapist used were duplicates of some we had at home. He had completely mastered them in our sessions and absolutely rattled off the names of the pieces as I handed them to him. Yet, at the center he rarely gave the therapist the satisfaction of identifying any of the symbols. Often, when the therapist supplied the proper name upon Evan's failure to respond, he would then echo the word as if he could only perform with prompting. At nursery school, too, Evan failed to use even the limited vocabulary he had. He never responded, for instance, to "hello" or "good morning."

I now realized that Evan deliberately assumed this air of ignorance and total lack of comprehension. Oh, I knew that he truly understood very little auditorily, but why did he pretend to those outside the family that his absence of understanding was complete? And why had he put on this performance for me with the colors? I had only the dimmest understanding of the reasons. A feeling of inadequacy was undoubtedly at the the bottom of Evan's strange behavior. At school he was the only one who did not belong to that seemingly unobtainable world of effortless communication. Rather than attempt to compete at something he was afraid he could never really succeed in, he chose not to compete at all. Perhaps he wished to reject relationships with other children, before they rejected him.

Evan was probably afraid that his therapist was going

to demand more of him than he was capable of giving. If he revealed to her that he was able to do certain things, might she not expect much more of him and then be disappointed when she found him wanting?

His performance with me was harder to understand. With the exception of the colors, Evan had worked enthusiastically to learn the things I had taught him. He was secure in the knowledge that I understood him, knew his limits and loved him dearly anyway. Apparently he felt the need to assert himself; prove that he could manipulate a situation if he chose. Children who do not understand speech must feel this need more than most. Not only are their lives planned and arranged for them without asking their preference, but they do not even have the privilege of being told what is going to happen next. Yes, they must have to show themselves and others that they *can* be master of a situation if they choose.

Evan had certainly shown me! Perhaps he was also motivated by a need to remind me not to get carried away. I mustn't become overconfident of his ability, for like the therapist and his peers, I would inevitably discover his inadequacy and be disappointed.

I was sure that this was a fairly accurate understanding of Evan's perhaps subconscious feelings. I knew I had to tread very carefully in the future to build his confidence that nothing would be demanded of him that he was not capable of. I would have to watch him closely so that, at the first indication he was raising his defenses, I could back away before we again fell into this psychological pit. His perseveration was what had made climbing out so difficult. Inadequacy and a need to assert himself had put us there in the beginning, but once the pattern of stubborn resistance was established, the pattern itself became the cause of his failure.

I had learned much from this experience. Evan had learned something too, however reluctantly: During our lesson period it was *I* who would be the ultimate judge of what we would do and what we would not do. However much I might compromise with him outside our daily sessions, it was I who would control the direction of our lessons.

I must never allow him to think that I doubted this for a moment. If Evan thought he could get away with choosing what he would or would not learn, the result could be disastrous. With this latest success we had jumped the first and greatest hurdle. I had asserted my authority.

The next afternoon when I got out the colored triangles I arranged them in a wheel as I had been doing and then said, "Evan? Do you want to put the blocks away in the drawer?"

I wanted to show him how brief we could make the less pleasant exercises if he cooperated.

Evan reached for the red block.

"What's this?" I asked, holding it with my finger.

"Red," said Evan matter-of-factly, and after putting the block away, clapped his hands as we had done the previous day. He picked up the yellow block and volunteered "yellow" without any prompting. He did equally well with the remaining blocks with the exception of the blue one. I knew he was truly not sure of that color yet. The bluff was over as far as colors were concerned. From that day onward we did our color exercise in this same quick way until he was sure of them.

Our educational program at this point was naturally evolving into its second subphase, although I was, of course, unaware of this. I only knew that Evan was steadily progressing and that the more he learned the more there was for him to learn. I had been organizing his lessons into three general categories: vocabulary, concepts and puzzle work. These latter two had now each given birth to a new and separate subject of study.

We had repeatedly gone through the simple counting of his blocks as one of Evan's exercises in concepts, and I now felt it was time to expand the flank of attack on the idea of numbers. Evan could count to ten orally fairly well. He usually omitted a number or two, but his finger did not sequentially touch each block as he did so. It might hit the first block two or three times and completely skip some or many of the others. He obviously did not understand the quantitative concept of numbers. Still, I felt that he did have a vague idea that numbers were associated in some way with amounts. I was using the two number toys we had given him for Christmas but so far with little success. Nevertheless, I hoped that the repeated methodical counting involved in these different games—always with Evan's finger being touched to each object as the counting progressed—would eventually produce the light of comprehension. I was using my "familiarization" theory here but with unaccustomed vigor, in an attempt to speed up the process. By forcing so pronounced and constant an awareness of the concept upon him, I hoped to hasten the understanding.

Evan had learned to recognize different shapes so quickly from his plastic blocks that it occurred to me he might just as easily learn to recognize numbers from some such three-dimensional objects. Finding nothing that suited my purpose in the stores, I bought several different colored sponges and proceeded to cut each into a large number. Initially I presented the *1* and the *2* to him. When he could differentiate between these and properly identify each, I presented the *3* and so on up to number *6*. To emphasize the relationship between the numbers themselves and the amounts they symbolized, I cut up the leftover pieces of sponge into small squares. One pink square was presented with the pink number *1,* two blue squares were presented with the blue *2,* and so on. Later, as I felt I was failing to really convey the quantitative idea of numbers to Evan, I used these little squares in a different way. Using a small cup, I had Evan pick up each miniature sponge and deposit it in the cup as we slowly counted together. After we had finished each counting, I would then say, "*How* many sponges?" Then I would supply the answer, "*three* sponges," to get across the idea that the last number mentioned signified the amount. We used only five sponges in this exercise, for I was trying to present my idea in as simple and basic a way as possible. At this time, to avoid oversaturating Evan with number exercises, I discontinued our efforts with the squares-and-pegs game, and just left this toy in his room.

A new category had also evolved from our work with puzzles, or at least I felt that it had. As Evan had learned to see the puzzle pieces as representations of objects, I had hopefully redoubled my effort to interest him in picture books. Searching in several different places, I found that the best books for my purpose were also the least expensive and usually could be found in the dime store or even the grocery store. These were the most elementary of picture books and were meant to be First Books for toddlers. The background of each page was white and carried pictures of individual objects, each clearly and simply outlined. A ball, a horse, a shoe—each object looked as if you could almost lift it off the page.

94

I found that Evan *could* recognize many of these objects, and soon we were further expanding his vocabulary with the aid of several of these picture books. I discovered, somewhat later, that he was able to see the more complex, paintinglike pictures as the scenes they represented. No longer were such pictures merely varicolored paper. His visual perception seemed completely normal now! Had a new pathway been laid in his brain? I was to ponder this question again and again. I was certain that the puzzles had been the means by which he had made the transition from perceiving three-dimensional objects to recognizing their two-dimensional representations.

With Evan's sharpened visual acuity, we were able to begin a new subject, which I thought of simply as *paperwork*. In a large writing tablet I carefully drew a square, a circle, a triangle and a rectangle. At once Evan was able to identify these. I was extremely excited, for it meant that I could teach him to recognize many more shapes and later numbers and letters on paper. Up to that point, my method of teaching had been confined to three-dimensional objects.

Also during our paperwork period I put a crayon in Evan's fingers and, guiding his hand, helped him to draw large circles and long "straight" lines. I repeated the word "circle" slowly, as we drew our lopsided spheres, and said "straight *line*" sharply as our crayon streaked down the page. Evan was gradually able to make a semblance of a circle on his own and then, eventually, a line. I found that he could only make the latter vertically by starting at the top of the paper and jerking his hand downward.

Our vocabulary period had expanded at a gratifyingly rapid pace. As Evan had learned to identify everything in his room long ago, I had been taking him on "house tours" during this section of our studies. Holding his hand—to remind him that this was a field trip and school was not out—I taught him to name every piece of furniture and most of the accessories in the house, and now I was teaching him to identify the rooms themselves. "What *room* is this?" as I made a sweeping gesture in each. "Bedroom? Living room? Hall room? Kitchen room?" In order to find household objects he did not yet know by name, I was reduced to opening cabinets and drawers and appraising their contents.

In our daily trips to school and the center, I had taught him the names for at least the most obvious things we saw along the way. We had started with "tree," "grass," "street" and "sidewalk," stopping to touch and name each as we walked. We had gone on to "house," "fence," "flower," "truck," "bus" (he already knew "car"), "sign" and so forth. We were now getting into more confusing terms: "building," for instance. I did not attempt to explain to Evan that a house was a type of building. The language required for such an explanation was beyond him. I merely designated any structure that was not a house, a "building." "Ground" was another problem word. Since Evan already knew "grass," "street," etc., I did not want to undermine his confidence in these terms. I found a grassless plot of earth and identified it as "ground." Then pointing upwards, I exclaimed "sky!" I hoped that by teaching him these two terms at the same time I would suggest the idea of opposites. Later, when I taught Evan "up" and "down," I would be able to carry this idea a step further. "*Up* in the sky" and "*down* on the ground" were phrases that would help all four concepts click into place.

It can be easily seen that I was getting into the problem of synonyms. I had always been taught in school that English is one of the most difficult and confusing of languages and I now understood, as I never had before, the annoying reality of this fact. It seemed to me that practically everything had two or three names.

96

It takes a great effort for the aphasic child to make the connection in his mind between an object and its name, and if he is confronted with several different names for one object—*e.g.*, "sofa," "couch," "davenport"—he can become so confused he may never make the connection at all. My solution to this problem generally was to present a synonym long after the original connection was established. For months Evan had been routinely pointing out the brown earth plot, declaring "ground." One day I stopped and said, "Yes, ground—*dirt!*" This utterance became a daily ritual until the two words were firmly related in Evan's mind.

I made one glaring omission in teaching Evan his "outdoor" vocabulary. I was afraid to point out the sun to him and give it a name, for I did not wish to center his attention on it. I had no means of warning him of the dangers involved in staring at the spectacular orb, and I was terrified that he might try to study it and become blinded.

Since I was running out of tangible everyday sources for new nouns, Evan's new ability to identify objects in picture books was a welcome aid to vocabulary lessons. I bought a simple primary picture dictionary and used this in addition to his toddler books. It was a big step for him to be able to learn to identify objects from representative illustrations. It opened up a whole new world of objects to be learned: things we did not have much or any personal access to. It was from a picture that I finally taught him the word "sun."

Now that we had put the trauma of learning colors behind us, our concept period had become steadily productive. I cut large squares, circles and triangles from plain white paper, along with their tiny counterparts. With these as aids, I taught Evan "big and little" in a few days. In teaching a concept it was of utmost importance to make sure that there was only one unknown differential. For instance, if Evan had not been sure of his colors or shapes and the paper cutouts had been multicolored, he would have had no way of knowing whether "big" referred to the size, the shape or the color. It would seem to be a matter of obvious common sense, but it is surprisingly easy to assume that the specific differential we are referring to will automatically be the one the child is most aware of. When Evan easily identified the "big and little" squares, rounds and triangles in his second lesson, I used his toys to enlarge upon the concept. I paired up two toy cars, two balls, two blocks. As I picked up one of the cars, I would say, "Is this car *big* or *little*, Evan? *Big* car or *little* car?" Always the greatest problem was posing the question so that he understood it. By mentioning both "big" and "little," Evan knew what it was I was asking for. The word "size" was meaningless, as yet. With white paper strips and then pencils and candles, Evan quickly learned "long and short." "Tall" was saved for a later date: another near-synonym!

We were now working on positions in space. Putting Evan's teddy bear at my chest, I would say, "Evan, where is bear?" Then I would supply the answer myself at first: "*In front of* Mama." With the bear at my back: "*Now*, where is bear? *Behind* Mama." I hoped to teach Evan to understand the word *where* by this activity, too.

Altogether, then, our daily lessons now included five categories or subjects: vocabulary, concepts, paperwork, numbers and still, for a time, puzzles. Such an impressive curriculum may suggest the idea of a four- or five-hour day, but actually we worked for thirty to forty minutes per afternoon.

I had wanted to be sure that Evan actually used the newly acquired knowledge in some way, in order that it not be forgotten and lost. I found that this did not necessarily doom us to boringly endless recitations. The shapes and colors, for example, were incorporated into other lessons; indeed, had become a useful vehicle for the teaching of other concepts. He was, of course, "read-ing" the shapes daily in his paperwork exercise, but they could also be used as known constant factors in demon-strating other differentials—"*big* square, *little* square." Similarly, concepts such as *long* and *short* were more easily taught when colors were known—"The *red* block is long, the *blue* block is short." I was able to see that he retained his hard-earned vocabulary and concepts by a system of reviewing and testing. I began curtailing the "house tours" to one a week, then to one every two weeks; and finally they became only occasional events. I found that Evan retained almost everything he learned. His identifications were automatic: a reflex action. I felt that I was succeeding in my intention to make this first basic knowledge a *part* of him.

I was getting a fascinating look at the workings of the human mind, an opportunity few people have. A normal child learns so naturally and automatically that we are, for the most part, quite unaware of the highly complex processes that are so rapidly taking place. Because of Evan's impaired ability to comprehend language, I saw these processes going on, as it were, in slow motion. We have all heard or made references to the "wonders of the human brain," and I, like everyone else, have nodded in affirmative recognition of the miraculous nature of this mysterious organ. But I had never really realized how truly incredible some of its most taken-for-granted func-tions are. It seemed to me as I proceeded to drill infor-mation and understanding into Evan's mind, that this was the natural way for children to learn. The remarka-ble thing was that most children absorbed the most com-plicated sort of knowledge without anyone bothering to teach it to them.

Strange that I had never marveled over the fact that Cindy and Wendy as toddlers had somehow learned the meaning of hundreds of words. I had never gone about our home touching and naming pieces of furniture for their benefit. Yet they had known the name for every piece. Nor had I demonstrated verbs. How had they learned such things? "Go into my bedroom and get my purse, it's time to go the store," I would say, and they would immediately set out to accomplish the mission. How had they learned all those words and concepts? To have independently learned the word "bedroom" now seemed astonishing, but how about "*my* bedroom"? And there was "go," "my purse," "store," and—Heavens!— "into" and "time." At the age of two or so they had learned to understand more language than I had in three years of high school and college French study. And I had never even had to learn concepts—just words!

One might assume that because Evan knew the words for most of the objects around him and had learned many of the basic verbs, and some adjectives, he would have made great progress in verbal communication. Such was not the case. He still lacked most of the concepts concerning the use of language. With the exception of the questions "What's this?" and "What am I doing?" which were used for the most basic identification, Evan really was not aware of the existence of questions. He did not realize that language was used to obtain desired information or to convey thoughts or hopes or emotions to another. Also, even though he could now answer the question "What's this?" it had not dawned upon him that he could also ask that question and find out something he wanted to know.

I suppose that if I had read the latter sentence before my experience in working with Evan, it would sound to me as if the child concerned was rather stupid. Surely, if the child understood the question well enough to answer it time after time, it would occur to him that he could ask it! I realized by now, however, that things were not that simple. The damaged portion of his brain, which controlled speech, was concerned with far more than just words. We had laid one pathway to the language center. "What's this?" was a sound stimulus for the automatic identification of something or other. A quite different pathway would have to be made before Evan could understand that he could satisfy his own curiosity verbally.

Outside our lesson periods I began to work on his conversational skills by expanding his ability to answer questions. As he sat at the kitchen table munching a sandwich, I asked, "What are *you doing?*" Then I supplied the answer: "*Eating.*"

Again I said, "Evan! What are *you doing?*" and hinted

at what I wanted him to say. "E-e-eat . . ." When he failed to respond, I again supplied "eating." I asked the question again and again. When Evan, as was his habit, echoed the *question,* I said, "No-*uh uh*-no-. E . . . e . . . eat . . ."

When Evan said "eating," I again asked the question, once more hinting at the proper response: "E . . . e . . . e . . ."

When Evan said "eating," more confidently this time, I exclaimed, "*Fine-yes,* that's right! *Now,* let's try it again! Evan! What are *you doing?*" Again, I prompted him. "E . . ." After a great deal of this, I finally got Evan to reply "eating" to my question, without any coaching. We repeated this question and answer at meals, for a couple of days, until Evan was sure of the proper response.

On the third day, during his bath, I asked, "Evan, what are *you doing?*" As I had known it would be, his response was "eating."

"No," I said. "No. What are you doing? *Taking a bath.*"

We had to go through the same procedure as we had with "eating" before Evan was finally able to reply "taking a bath" to my query. For a week or two I asked him my question at every meal and during each bath. Now he had to think before he answered; he could not respond mechanically. There were two possible answers to my question, and he had to make certain connections in his mind before he could give the appropriate response.

After a couple of weeks I asked the same question when he was sitting quietly—for once—in a chair. Although I had to help him with the answer, "sitting," the process did not take so long this time. I kept asking him my question as he was engaged in different activities. After he had gained a degree of assurance in giving trained responses, he eventually was able to give his first spontaneous answer. I had asked him what he was doing as he was drinking a glass of water, and his answer was

102

simply "drink." I watched the wheels turn in his mind as first the meaning of my question registered. Then he determined what function he was engaged in and, finally, he found a word to verbalize that function. A new connection had definitely been made!

This was to be the method I would repeatedly use in establishing Evan's conversational concepts. I would equip him with trained, mechanical words or phrases to make him able to participate in a verbal exchange. After a while the rehearsed words became meaningful and, eventually, spontaneous and changeable. For example, I taught him to say, "I want a cookie, please, Mama" instead of the old "want-some-cookie?" At first he would use this phrase only in requesting a cookie or the two or three other things he had been specifically trained to use this sentence with. Eventually, however, he realized that any other desire was almost certain to be granted if he fished this sentence from his mental file and inserted the proper word into it. We might be passing the ten-cent electrical rocking horse in front of the grocery store and his first excited reaction would, as usual, be "Horse! Horse! Want some horse?" Then he would hesitate, the momentary expression of concentration in his eyes revealing his rapid search for a sentence that would please me. "I want a horse, please, Mama!" he would finally exclaim. Learning the basic sentence form had taken more than a week, but once learned it could be used for a hundred different things!

One Saturday at lunch, Don took a banana from its bowl on the counter.

"Want some 'nana?" Evan asked, reaching for the fruit.

"No, Evan," I coached, "Not 'want some banana.' *I . . . I . . .*"

"I want a 'nana, please, Mama," Evan dutifully declared, directing his statement to Don.

"Mama! I'm *Daddy!*" Don reminded Evan, amused.

103

I could see by his expression that Evan realized what was wrong with his sentence, but changing it was not as easy as it might seem. Except for the one changeable word, the sentence was automatic.

"I want a 'nana, please, Ma . . ." he tried again. I held my breath.

"I want a 'nana, please—*Daddy!*" he managed, finally, with some effort.

I breathed again. He could do it! He could take apart the words in a sentence and analyze them. A sentence was no longer one continuous sound stimulus. He was getting that basic idea of *putting words together.*

From that day on we made a point of seeing that different members of the family offered him different things, forcing his mind to *think,* to *analyze,* to *improvise* upon this one sentence. "I want a cupcake, please, Cindy." "I want a orange, please, Wendy." We knew he was learning the method he would need in constructing a thousand other future sentences.

It was like programming a computer, I told my husband. Evan's brain, or at least the part of it I was working with, seemed completely separate from Evan himself. I had to program this portion of his mind, feed into it all necessary information and set up certain connections in order to make the system operational. Evan's personality was in no way integrated with this system any more than it was with his hand or foot. There was certainly nothing mechanical about Evan himself! He was bright and affectionate and charming. The portion of his brain in question was merely a tool he needed to function normally, as he needed his hands.

I believe that having a handicapped child gives one a sharper awareness of the existence of the soul, the id or whatever we want to call it. That essence of a person which transcends his faculties. Normally, as we view people, we see even their most mechanical functions as a

104

part of the conglomerate whole we call their personalities—*e.g.,* their manner of speech, their graceful or plodding or rapid way of moving. But a parent whose child lacks, or is impaired in, one of his faculties is very conscious of the separateness of this and other faculties from the child himself. Consequently the parent gains an insight and understanding not necessarily confined to the difficulties of his own child. I should never think of mentally retarded individuals in quite the same way again, for instance. I would not see such a person as a *less intelligent* individual, but as one whose thinking apparatus does not function well. A question of semantics? Perhaps to some, but to me the difference in wording underscores a completely different point of view.

It was always necessary to indicate in some way to Evan when one was about to say something meant for his ears. That meaningless "hum" of conversation had to be interrupted in order to get him to tune in. This problem belongs in the general category of dysynchronization. Although Evan's concentration was constantly fading out during our lessons, I never really found it a great problem to deal with. A sharp "Evan!" and perhaps a snap of my fingers was usually all it took to refocus his attention to where it belonged. If this was not enough, then touching him, firmly grasping his shoulder or taking his chin in my hand did the trick. As our lessons went on, his concentration span increased and I realized that this alone would have made our sessions worthwhile.

Everything, in fact, was going well with our program at home. All systems were definitely "go." I felt that, from a strictly academic viewpoint, Evan was learning everything that he should be at his age; indeed, was forging ahead. His vocabulary was now quite extensive, and if his understanding of ordinary daily speech was progressing at a slow pace, this in itself did not worry me. We had known that language, after all, was Evan's specific handicap. I had not even expected that he would be able to learn words and their meanings so readily and easily. The important thing was that Evan's intellect was developing and progressing in spite of the handicap. He could not learn many of the ordinary, everyday things his peers did: that interesting people existed a "long time ago," that certain holidays or fun "surprises" would be coming up; nor could he know if something was "beautiful" or "ugly." If he could keep abreast of his peers in required academic knowledge and skills, however, then he would eventually be able to take his proper place in the world. He could catch up on the other things later. When his language skills got to that point where he could communicate with others, he would not find himself still separated from them by an unbridgeable intellectual chasm.

Evan was still putting on his I-don't-know-anything act both at school and with his therapist. I winced when I watched him staring blankly at squares, triangles and the like in school, as if he hadn't the least idea of what his teacher was talking about. His therapist was working with him on things that Evan and I had covered months before at home and he knew totally. Occasionally he would identify things for her; but for the most part, he feigned ignorance.

"He's putting you on, you know," I would tell her. I brought her a list of the words he knew and the things he had learned and could identify. I don't think she exactly *disbelieved* me, but she may have thought I was exaggerating a bit (or *quite* a bit). If *I* had been her, *I* don't think I would have believed me! After all, there sat Evan, returning her queries about the identity of an animal, a color, etc. with a vacuous stare. She went back to the elementary rings and puzzles.

I was in a frightening position. I had become indispensable. If Evan was going to make it, it would have to be through me. We all like to feel important and needed; we may even think that we would like to be considered indispensable, but we don't truly want to be this. We are, after all, human, and as such, subject to the whims of fate. If anything should happen to me, I thought, Evan would be lost. Not saddened and confronted with a more difficult childhood as the girls would be, but *lost!* So far, he refused to attempt to learn from anyone else. I doubted greatly that he could transfer my role to another in the event of my disappearance. My death *would* be to him a disappearance. There would be no way to explain such an occurrence to him. He would think that I had simply abandoned him, and probably retreat into his shell forever.

Uneasy over even the remote possibility of some mischance causing such an unspeakable tragedy, I began to be unaccustomedly cautious with myself. I had always been casual about medical checkups, sometimes stretching the intervals between to two or more years; I now saw the doctor religiously. On car trips with my husband, I became an overly anxious passenger, often prompting Don to inquire whether I had received my copilot's license yet.

It was no way to live, I knew. I had thought I would be able to relax when I saw Evan making such intellectual progress. I knew now that I could rest only when he was learning from others in the same way he did from me. I was certain this would happen, eventually. When he reached a certain point in his knowledge and ability to communicate, he would feel confident enough to open up and allow others to know his mind.

I only needed enough time. If I were granted that, I would probably live to the age of ninety-seven and never worry about my mortality again.

**M**y programming of Evan's language center for conversation began to show noticeable results. I taught him to respond to the sound stimulus "What's your name?" with "Evan," and to "How are you?" with "Fine." Since people were virtually always asking him these questions, his new ability to answer them was very useful, as well as gratifying. In the beginning Evan wore an expression of startled surprise as he recognized these sounds coming from the lips of strangers and he found himself able to respond to them. Participating with outsiders in a verbal exchange was a new experience!

Although Evan knew his own name, he did not know the meaning of the word "name," and certainly not the meaning of "what," "is," or "your." It was through his own repeated, mechanical response to the same sound that the sound itself—"What-is-your-name?"—began to take on meaning for him. He also made his first associations with the single word "name."

I was attempting to teach him to answer "yes" and "no" to simple questions, but this was pretty much beyond him as yet. We did make a small step in this direction by sort of tacking a "yes" onto his habitual echo. If one said, "Evan, are you eating a sandwich?" he would echo "eating a sandwich." Although his echo was automatic, it carried a more meaningful tone when he was actually engaged in the action being mentioned, as if he understood that he was confirming a question.

"Evan! Say 'Yes, I'm eating a sandwich,'" I coached.

"Yes, I'm (doing so and so)" became another mechanical response in Evan's repertoire. It sounded good, but if anyone was prompted to playfully tease him the result was unfortunate.

"My, what curly blond hair! You should be a girl! Are

109

you a little girl?" A well-intentioned stranger might mischievously ask.

"Yes, I'm a little girl," would come the quite sober, automatic response.

Still, for the most part, these conditioned-reflex answers made Evan seem more like other children and strongly made him feel more a part of things. Also, I knew that every time he participated in such a verbal exchange the words took on a little more meaning for him. I could almost see yet another tiny brain cell fastening itself to a growing line of them until a new pathway was established.

Evan and I were in the habit of lunching at a little restaurant every Friday after therapy. This was his very favorite thing to do, and it had a far more important effect upon him than even I realized at the time. It amounted to a weekly lesson in public behavior. Upon our arrival in front of the restaurant and before getting out of the car, I would take Evan's chin in my hands and stress that he was to be a good boy. Once inside the restaurant, we would go to the ladies' room to wash our hands, and I would again make a point of emphasizing that he was to be "good." If, while at our table, he began to throw a tantrum when something did not fit into the expected pattern, I would remind him that he was to be a "good boy" or we would "go home," and I might even start to rise and collect my things. I managed to get my point across to him although I did have a few embarrassing experiences. It was well worth it, however, and much easier to give him such public lessons while he was still quite a little boy. He learned to behave in public places with a self-control he never showed at home. His only original incentive for exercising this control was his overwhelming desire to stay in the restaurant, for he had no inhibitions about making a spectacle of himself. Behaving himself when out became a natural habit, and after several months of "restaurant training," Don and I found that we could take Evan almost anywhere with never (well, all right, *rarely*) a problem.

Evan's lessons were going so well that I was having trouble keeping my teaching plan at least one jump ahead of his learning. How I wished for some kind of guidebook! It was hard to set out to teach a child "everything" and try to present the material included in this vague category, in its order of importance. I took to carrying a notepad everywhere with me so that when a word or concept Evan should know occurred to me, I could jot it down.

The vocabulary lessons that had been so easy to program at first now required some strategic planning. It seemed to me that I had taught Evan the words for almost everything in his surroundings. Had I really, I asked myself, or was I overlooking obvious things? Perhaps I was too close to our work and unable to see the forest for the trees! As this metaphoric cliché passed aimlessly through my mind, I suddenly realized what our next step should be. Of course! The forest and the trees! I had taught Evan the names of the "trees" but not of the "forests." He now comprehended the words "man," "woman," "girl," "boy," "baby," but not "people." He could identify almost any type of food but he did not know the word "food" itself. I needed to teach Evan categorical terms.

I had to be very careful about my method of presenting category words, for such words involved a concept which he must first understand. If I were simply to point to a chair, a table and a sofa and say "furniture," Evan would have no idea of what I was attempting to convey. He was now confident that he knew the names for these individual objects and might think I was trying to tell him something about the texture, the shape—anything!

I collected a pile of magazines and a large art paper

111

pad and set to work with scissors and paste. I would begin with four categories: people, animals, furniture and food. I cut out all the good pictures I could find that belonged in these categories and mounted them on four heavy sheets of art paper according to their proper groups. With these homemade charts I managed to get my idea across to Evan rather easily.

"Evan, these are *people,*" I would say to him, picking up the chart with pictures of men, women and children pasted onto it. "These are *all people.*" It was both desirable and necessary to teach him the word "all" at this time, too. I touched every picture on the chart, asking, "What's this?" When Evan had identified each one, I would say, "You're *right,* Evan. Man, woman, girl, boy, baby—these are *all people!*"

I followed the same procedure with the animal, furniture and food charts. After three lessons or so I began to ask him for the category term as I picked up each chart. "What's this, Evan? These are all——. Evan, these are all p. . . peop. . ." When Evan was able to identify each chart, I used an additional method to drive the concept home. Pointing to his bed, I would ask, "What's that, Evan?"

"Bed!" was the positive answer.

"You're *right,* Evan, it's a bed, but it's f. . . f . . . fur . . . *furniture.*" At first it was necessary to supply the answers myself, for Evan had no way of knowing what question I was asking. When he did understand what I was driving at, I made a point of testing him on the categories during our daily routine until I felt they were well established in his mind.

"What's this, Evan?"

"Apple."

"You're *right,* it's an apple, but an apple is——"

"Food," Evan was, at length, able to answer.

Although I had planned to make more charts of

categorical groups, I never made more than the original four. I found that Evan had absorbed the concept of categories so well that I was thereafter able to convey this idea verbally. "Plate, cup, saucer—these are *all dishes.*'

By now Evan had learned to identify most of the objects in his picture books. There were certain terms I did not bother with for now: "king and queen," for example. These terms required the kind of abstract, verbal explanation that was simply beyond Evan, and I did not waste precious time on futile endeavors. There was so much important, basic knowledge he *could* learn. We would spend our time on that and worry about less important ideas later.

Now I began to use his picture books to increase his verb vocabulary by teaching him the functions associated with the various objects portrayed.

"What is this?"

"Hammer!""And what do you *do* with a hammer?"

"Pound!" In the beginning, of course, we went through our usual routine. I answered my own question at first and then hinted at the response until Evan knew it and understood what I was after.

I could not always be sure that he understood the exact meaning of each verb he was learning, but I felt that by associating an action word with a certain object or objects, he would *come* to understand it. He realized very quickly, from my method of presentation, that the words he was learning symbolized *functions.* With each picture I always first asked the very familiar "What's this?" to establish the object's identity. When Evan had answered correctly, I would nod emphatically. "*Yes,* that's *right,* it's a *hammer.*" Confident that the object's name was no longer in question, he realized that the second and different sounding query, "What do you do with a ——?" dealt with something else. A few of the verbs were familiar. "What do you do with an apple?" "Eat." Since he

113

recognized these as actions, he soon realized that the new question was always concerned with an action. Our extra-lesson conversational work with questions and answers concerning functions—"What are you doing?" "Eating."—had already underscored the idea of *action* as opposed to object. The new verb lessons not only enlarged upon this idea but provided him with a means of methodically learning new and unfamiliar verb vocabulary.

An important part of these verb lessons was teaching Evan the words for the functions associated with his own sense organs. As I touched both of his ears, I would ask, "What's this? What are these?"

"Ears," he was able to answer. I had previously taught him the words for "eyes," "ears," "nose" and "mouth" during his baths.

"What do you *do* with your ears?"

"Hear," Evan learned to respond.

Each day I would ask him for the name and the function of his eyes, ears, nose and mouth. Only he could know whether he truly understood the meaning of the words "see," "hear," "smell" and "eat," but getting these terms firmly linked with their particular organs almost completely assured that he would come to understand them.

Concept study, because of its very nature, proceeded much more slowly than simple vocabulary learning. We usually started this segment of our daily lesson with a quick drill on previously learned concepts of size: *big, little; long, short.* We were still working with spatial positions: *behind, in front of, beside, below, above, up, down,* etc. I demonstrated some of these conceptual terms with blocks, teddy bears, anything handy, putting the toy first *behind* Mama, then *behind* Evan, etc. This work with spatial concepts was particularly difficult as there seemed to be so many words to convey like or similar ideas.

Take "up," "high," "above," "over," "top," for example; or "down," "below," "beneath," "under." I avoided confusing Evan by using these words interchangeably, but instead, chose the most commonly used terms and grouped them in *sets,* teaching each set separately with a different activity. "In front of," "behind," "beside," "over" and "under" were taught with the placement of the toy in relation to *Mama, Evan* or a piece of furniture. "The block is *behind* the chest." "Top," "bottom" and "middle" were easily taught with the aid of different chests of drawers. "Up and down" were likewise simple to demonstrate. The ceiling was "up," the floor was "down"; the sky was "up," the ground was "down." Later, I tested Evan on the latter two terms by lifting a toy high in the air and then lowering it to the floor. "Evan, the car is u... u... up." This initially caused some confusion as to whether I was asking for "up" or "over," "down" or "under," but once the words had originally been learned separately, the confusion was more over the meaning of the question rather than over the words themselves. "High," "low," "above" and "below" were taught by tacking these words to "up" and "down" once Evan was certain of the latter terms. "The ceiling is *up,* Evan. Up *high.*" We did a little work with the words "in" and "out" by shifting toys in and out of boxes, but I found that Evan already seemed to understand these terms fairly well.

Much of our actual work with concepts was now incorporated into that section of the lesson I rather unimaginatively referred to as paperwork. This area of study had become the most exciting part of our lessons, for we were actually involved in prereading. Since I had found that Evan had developed the ability to recognize squares, rounds, triangles and rectangles on paper, I had gradually added a star, a heart, a cross, an oval, a diamond, an arrow, etc., to a special page in our writing

115

tablet. He could now identify quite a number of shapes and symbols. Occasionally I would make a new page of shapes, putting them in different order to ensure that Evan did not merely recite by consecutive memory rote.

I had transferred the reading of number symbols from number period to paperwork period, due to an unforeseen disaster befalling my laboriously executed sponge numbers. Suddenly aware of an unaccustomed quiet in the house one afternoon, I hastened to Evan's room where I found him sitting in the midst of a pile of minute pink, blue, yellow and green sponge fragments. Somehow he had managed to get the box of sponge numbers down from his closet shelf and had apparently been having a delightful time tearing them into as many pieces as possible. Since we had already been working with the identification of shapes and symbols on paper, and also since I was somewhat less than enthralled with the idea of undertaking once again the tedious task of cutting numbers from the rubbery substance, I continued his number recognition lessons on paper. We had gone as far as number 6 with the sponge digits, and I found that after a couple of lessons he could recognize these in our writing tablet. I had to be very careful about my formation of the numbers, and I made them rather large at first. I prepared one page in the tablet with the numbers in their proper consecutive order and another—which I changed occasionally—with the digits jumbled up. Each lesson I had Evan read both so that he would remain cognizant of the correct counting order, and yet not depend upon memory rote in recognizing the symbols. I added a new number to the pages every few days, and Evan could soon readily identify number symbols to twelve.

With Evan's shape and number reading going so well, I saw no reason why he should not be learning his letters. Although he was now able to learn *new* shapes and numbers in two-dimensional black and white, I did not want to begin teaching him his letters in this fashion. I felt that, as with the shapes and numbers, he could more easily relate to and learn them if I presented them initially in some unique way. I sensed that it was important for him to be able to hold each letter in his hand; that sense of touch, that ability to hold something and lift it close, helping to make that connection that *this* is an *A*. I cast around for something I could use for my purpose. We had some small plastic letters which could be magnetically affixed to a board but I did not especially like them. I felt their shapes were too bulky and closed up, and for a child with possible visual-perception problems, I wanted to be sure that the letters were as much like the conventional printed ones as possible. I entertained, fleetingly, the idea of cutting them out of felt, but I was afraid such a task might take too long and I was impatient to begin. At length, I remembered an old ABC animal book the girls had had when they were small. I had resurrected it for Evan, but as he had shown no interest, the book had again been gathering dust on a closet shelf. Hopefully, I took the book down and opened it. Yes, memory had served me correctly. The letters were simply formed and executed in several different bright colors. Each page bore both the capital and small letter which stood for the particular animal pictured there. Taking my scissors, I cut a square around each letter, making small flash cards of them. The large and small letters were related by color: *i.e.*, *A* and *a* were red, *B* and *b* were blue and so on. Putting the letters in a small box, I waited expectantly for Evan's afternoon lesson. We would start with the first three letters of the alphabet, learning the large and small case letters at once, for I had read that these should be taught together.

I had been putting Evan's prereading work—paperwork period—at the beginning of our sessions; I felt he was at his sharpest then for the type of visuo-oral memorization involved. So, bringing out the little box of letters was the first thing I did this day.

"These are *letters,* Evan. These are *all letters!"* I told him. It was important to make a point of repeatedly referring to everything by their categorical names, since this was Evan's only way of learning them. It was something so obvious that it would have been easy to forget. I realized this when Evan was becoming quite proficient in the identification of shapes and it suddenly occurred to me that he did not know what the word "shape" meant. Now I prefaced each daily learning exercise with the same type of explanatory phrase I had been using in the teaching of categories. "These are *numbers.* These are all *numbers!"* or "*shapes.*" These are *all shapes!"* Taking both the large and the small *A*'s, I held them up for Evan to see across the table. "*A,* letter *A,*" I announced.

Then, laying the capital letter to my right facing him, I said, "Big *A,*" and placing the small letter to my left, "Little *a.*"

I followed the same procedure with letters *B* and *C,* identifying the letters, then differentiating the large and small letters and putting them in their proper piles on the table. I ran through this entire routine a couple of more times and then started asking Evan to identify each letter as I held both the large and small symbols up. He got *A* and *B* that first afternoon and even began to repeat "Big *A,* little *a,*" etc. with me, as I placed the letters in their assigned groups. After three or four days, when Evan was able to readily identify the first three letters of the alphabet, I began to steadily add other letters, one at a time, to the group we worked with. As he mastered each new letter, we would go on to another. I did not thereafter give him the letters in alphabetical order but rather according to the degree of difference in shape. That is, I gave him letter *O* early but saved *Q* to be one of the last letters. I also spaced the teaching of *M* and *N* quite widely apart, as both the similar shape and sound might have caused confusion.

When Evan had learned ten or twelve letters, I printed them on a page in our reading tablet. Reading the letter page became a part of our exercises, although I still kept on with the colored letter cards until we had finished the alphabet.

Evan took a great interest and seemed to feel pride of accomplishment in this prereading work. He would get the tablet and letter cards from my closet in the evenings and indicate that he wanted me to drill him on the shapes, numbers and letters. He also began to get the tablet out at other odd times and sit and "read" aloud the various symbols independently, his chubby little finger moving down the pages.

"That book is meaningful to him," said my husband, when I expressed my delighted astonishment in seeing a child so eager to do noncompulsory "homework."

Yes, I thought to myself, Don had hit the nail exactly on the head. In Evan's world so little meant anything; ordinary conversation, television, books and newspapers the rest of us read—these were all things that we participated in and understood, but from which Evan was excluded. This pad of paper, however, held symbols that he understood, that he could recognize and identify. This book symbolized that part of his world in which he was proficient.

The "drawing" part of paperwork period had not been going well. Evan had learned to execute a semblance of a round shape and make a downward slash of the crayon for a straight line, but after two or three weeks at this work, his face had begun to assume that veiled expression reminiscent of our troubled time in color learning. When he started making round shapes when I asked for straight lines, and vice versa, I stopped this activity completely for a time. When he had misconstrued my directions for the third successive time, I could tell by his strange expression that the mistake was deliberate, and I realized that if I continued to ask him to do this same thing, I would only allow the defiant pattern to become more set. I was up against that same mysterious block I had encountered when teaching him colors, but this time I was able to use a little wisdom in handling it. Of primary importance was the fact that I was now able to see the problem in its true perspective. Whatever this block was, it was not an obstruction to all or most learning as I had feared when working with colors, or at least it certainly was not now. I no longer needed to worry whether I would be able to teach him or not. Our work, in most areas, was going far better than I had dared dream. Perhaps my stubborn persistence and breaking down of that barrier was necessary that first time. I cannot be certain. Colors was only the second abstract concept I had attempted to teach Evan. If I were to do it again, I would probably go on to other concepts, and only if I encountered that psychological block in most of them would I persist as stubbornly as I had before.

At any rate, such was certainly not the case now. Drawing was only only one area of our endeavor. It was not worth jeopardizing our excellent teacher-student rapport for this relatively minor matter. I therefore gave no sign of noticing that Evan was purposely defying me but simply ceased the drawing for several weeks. When I introduced it again, I avoided round circles and straight lines in an effort to avoid reactivating the same stubborn pattern. Instead, I helped him to attempt to draw fruit —oranges, apples, bananas, etc.—to make it seem like a brand-new activity. Still, drawing was not something Evan really liked and it would be quite a while before we did it on a steady basis. We would work at it as a part of our lessons for days or weeks and then drop it. I had continued to teach Evan his colors during paperwork period because of the obvious adaptability of the crayons to this purpose. He could now, triumphantly, name them all as I took them, one by one, from their box.

Number period was not especially productive either at this time. As mentioned, I had switched the reading of numbers to paperwork or prereading period, so the quantitative concept was now the only thing we were concentrating on during this lesson segment. Evan's oral counting was good but he did not yet seem to have absorbed the idea that numbers represented specific amounts—or had he? As in drawing, I began to feel that I was encountering silent resistance again.

Among other counting exercises, we still often worked with the cup and tiny sponges. I had gotten Evan to the place where he could pick each sponge up one at a time and place it in the cup, counting consecutively "One-two-three-four-five." But when I asked him "How many sponges?" he might say "four," "two" or anything *but* the last number counted. My firm confidence in his intellectual ability was making me extremely suspicious that he was again putting me on. We had done these various counting exercises so many times! Still, I could not be sure. The quantitative concept was quite an abstract one. Perhaps he really had not experienced the flash of comprehension yet. He had, however, rather suddenly learned to work the peg-and-squares-with-holes toy. Although this did not require verbal counting, it showed that he was now aware that five holes must be associated with five pegs, three holes with three pegs and so forth.

Since I suspected that I was perhaps confronted by the psychological obstruction, I began to treat it as that. I would drop counting altogether for a week or so and then reintroduce it in a new way using blocks, pins, anything. I was not hoping to fool him into thinking we were really doing anything different by this. Counting is too obviously always the same. Rather, I was hoping to give him a graceful way of giving in without losing face. If he were indeed being stubborn, then perhaps a new way of doing this same activity might allow him to pretend it was not the same. I put as much careful planning and effort into the presentation of number concepts as I could muster, for I felt that counting, unlike drawing, *was* of great importance at this time, and I could not simply forget about it.

With the growth of the amount of material to cover, I had eliminated puzzles from our afternoon curriculum, for I did not want our sessions to exceed forty minutes. Evan's attention usually began to wander if we went beyond this time limit, and I did not want him to associate boredom with the lessons. We worked with the puzzles in the evening, as we often did the little farm while playing his records. I was, however, adding a new activity at the conclusion of our afternoon lessons: the reading of stories. Evan had never listened to a story—indeed, *could* not. His understanding of language was nowhere near adequate, and this bothered me terribly. I had always strongly believed that reading to children was of utmost importance. Not only was it a primary source of education but it developed imagination, even molded character. Evan was most keenly disadvantaged in the area of imagination. He had none. At the age of four he did not even know what a story was. To hear about and relate to the experiences of another, real or imaginary, in another dimension of space and time was an idea not even conceived of by Evan. To simply wait until that uncertain day when he understood enough language to comprehend the idea of a story would, I felt, be a death blow to his intellect. If I could just get across to him the basic concept of what a story was, perhaps I could activate his curiosity enough to spur him into using his native intelligence in making some sense out of books.

I had searched the stores but had found that even the simplest story books were quite beyond Evan's auditory comprehension. Nursery rhymes were out of the question since they are so ambiguous. I had tried going through books with Evan, telling the stories in my own words. But this was most unsatisfactory. To carefully pick and choose words which he could understand and at the same time try to convey an idea or image with these words was almost impossible to do ad lib, to a child who was both so handicapped and so unaware of our purpose. I found it necessary to constantly hesitate while searching for phrases, and hesitation meant the loss of Evan's erratic attention.

I had to stop groping around and come up with some thoughtfully conceived method of conveying the story idea to Evan just as I had done with his other concepts. Hunting among the twenty-nine-cent books at the grocery and dime stores—the best sources of books full of good basic pictures—I ignored the text of the stories and chose books with illustrations I thought Evan could relate to most easily. One book was about a little blond boy, "Daniel," who looked much like Evan. The illustrations portrayed the boy eating, playing ball, pulling a wagon—in other words, engaged in actions Evan could recognize and relate to. I also chose *The Three Bears* since I wanted Evan to become at least familiar with the stories universally known by children. I found that the most beautifully illustrated books were not usually the best for my purpose: the simpler, less artistic pictures were better for ease of identification.

At home, starting with the book about Daniel, I cut out pieces of lined notebook paper and taped them over the printed text. This done, I proceeded to carefully print my own story on the blank paper. I did not attempt any sort of plot or real story line in the first effort; I merely put together very short sentences describing the pictures with words I knew Evan could understand. I included a very few words he could not comprehend, such as "said," "has," "he," etc., in the hope that with repeated readings he might pick up a rudimentary understanding or, at least, an awareness of these words. The first page portrayed Daniel sitting among his toys, and my words accompanying this illustration were simply, "Daniel is a little boy. Daniel has some nice toys. He has toy blocks, a toy train, a toy dog and a ball." My text for the other pages were similarly inspirational: "Daddy is a big man. Daddy pulls Daniel in the wagon. Daddy loves Daniel." Or "Daniel goes to sleep. He takes the toy dog to bed. Mama reads a book to Daniel." My aim was to get Evan to see Daniel as a little boy like himself who shared many things in common with him. I hoped Evan could identify with Daniel, and thus make a first step toward transporting himself and experiencing situations vicariously.

I was careful to print my words very plainly, knowing Evan could recognize many of the letters. Perhaps he would come to understand that these groups of letters were what prompted the words I would repeat so often. Even with his growing recognition of letters, he after all had no way of knowing what people were really doing when they scanned a printed page.

Since Evan became impatient and restless at the mere sight of a book during his leisure hours, I decided to include story time as the last item on our lesson agenda, when he was oriented toward concentrating on activities chosen *for* him rather than *by* him. Seating Evan beside me on top of the little work table so that he could see the pictures well, I read my own printed words slowly and distinctly, occasionally supplementing them with extra remarks for emphasis. "See, Evan, *Daniel* has a ball! *Evan* has a ball, too."

There was no flicker of interest that first day, nor the next nor the next. But on the fourth day Evan wanted to linger on the first page and study Daniel's "nice toys" more closely. I began the practice of asking Evan obvious questions about the book. "Who is that? What's this?" pointing to Daniel.

"Evan."

"No, it's not Evan. Who *is* it?"

After a while he answered, "Boy." It took some prompting before he could tell me the boy's name. Even when he could answer "Daniel" to my question on the identity of the boy on the first page, Evan was at a loss when asked to name this same boy on subsequent pages. This is not too puzzling when one remembers that Evan had no concept of a *story*. He had not yet grasped the idea of following a character through a series of adventures. Different pages must mean different people and different names to go with them. The fact that all the illustrations of Daniel looked so much alike was not enough to clear up Evan's confusion. For one thing, his visual perception could be off. More important, how could he know that because two illustrations looked alike they therefore represented the same person? Two red wagons might look alike but they were still different wagons. Insights we take so for granted are dependent upon the establishment of certain mental connections. The connection may be a small one, but the absence of it may prevent comprehension on an enormous scale. It would be tragically easy to miss pinpointing these missing connections in a child's brain and to conclude instead that he simply lacks intelligence.

In this case the connection was quite easy to establish. I followed my usual question-answer-prompting procedure. "Who is this? D. . . D. . . Dan. . ." at three or four different places in the book. Selecting a fifth page at random, I pointed again to a drawing of the little blond boy and asked "Who is this?"

"Daniel." Evan answered, somewhat uncertainly.

125

"That's *right,* Evan!" I exclaimed encouragingly. I turned to another page. "And who is this?"

"Daniel." replied Evan, confidently now.

He understood, I was certain. That flash of comprehension had occurred. I turned to still another page, then another and another, asking the same question. Evan's answer remained unchanged. These drawings of blond boys all represented "Daniel." Finally I gave him the ultimate test. "Who is that?" I asked again, this time pointing to Daniel's brown-haired little friend. Evan hesitated.

"Boy," he said finally.

No, he was not simply parroting the answer I had originally given him. The fact that he *could* differentiate between Daniel and his friend proved that Evan truly understood. Another mental pathway was now properly connected and ready for travel.

Thereafter with each new book, I always asked Evan to identify the central character or characters at different points in the story. I found that it was still necessary to do so in the beginning to establish the same basic concept that this book concerned the same person or persons throughout. Later on this routine seemed to be necessary more out of the need to focus his concentration on the story.

In a few days I added *The Three Bears* to our story hour. In rewriting this book, as with subsequent ones, I did not attempt to get across the actual plot. This would have been much too complex for Evan at this stage. Rather my purpose was to give him some familiarity with the characters and to teach him word-picture association.

I also considered the story reading another big step toward helping Evan understand normal conversation. Through repeatedly listening to the same sentences, the general sense of which he could grasp with the aid of the illustrations, he would probably absorb at least some vague comprehension of words such as I have previously mentioned: words like *say, said, does, has,* etc. These words were almost impossible to teach in regular vocabulary lessons; the enormous amount of time involved in attempting to illustrate them would have been prohibitive and the effort would, in all probability, have been futile. We of course used them in speaking to Evan, but he could not learn from ordinary daily conversation as others did. Hearing the words *read,* however, over and over, in the same unchanging sentences in the book was much more likely to force comprehension. Day after day he would hear the sentence, "Daniel has some nice toys." He would look at the picture of Daniel and his toys and be able to see and understand that Daniel *possessed* these toys as Evan did his own. After—how many?— repetitions of that same sentence, he would begin to get some understanding of the meaning of the word "has." I knew that when this began to happen I would probably not realize it. There would be no dramatic pointing to an object and exclaiming "has!" Rather, my knowledge of his comprehension would be delayed until sometime after the fact when he began to use the word himself.

Evan's reception of *The Three Bears* was cool, to say the least, but at the same time, he began to take a genuine interest in *Daniel.* About the third week or so, when I introduced *Little Red Riding Hood,* I noted that *The Three Bears* became almost as popular as *Daniel.* And so it went. As Evan grew used to a book, it began to seem like an old friend, especially when compared with a new one, and as his interest grew, so did his understanding of the stories themselves. We only had time to read two or three stories at a sitting, so after I had read Evan a book daily for about three weeks, I started to alternate it with another. By this system of juggling, I was able to give him a modestly wide variety of stories and at the same time not give up the all-important repetition. So successful were the story books, I was eventually able to do most of our reading during our evening hour, thus giving it the classification of play rather than work.

It was April once more. A full year had gone by since the discovery of Evan's handicap. So absorbed was I in the planning and accomplishment of each step in Evan's intellectual development, I hardly had time to fully appreciate the dramatic change that had taken place. From a child at about the eighteen-month-old level of mental achievement, Evan had become an eager and competent student already involved in some phases of learning which would not be required of his peers for a year or two. It was not yet time, however, to indulge in any feelings of triumph. Evan's progress was indeed almost our secret. He still gave little hint of his capabilities during his therapy sessions, but it seemed as if we might be at some sort of turning point here. His therapist had recently introduced a new set of picture cards to him and had sat stunned as Evan, interested for once, had readily identified the majority of them.

"How long has he been able to do that?" she asked me later, her face a study in puzzled amazement.

"Do what?" I had, with some embarrassment, attempted to keep her informed of the things Evan was able to do at home and he had long been identifying familiar objects from pictures.

"How long has he been able to name those things on the cards?"

"I guess for about three months or so," I answered, thinking back.

Since this incident the therapist had had a wholly new attitude toward Evan, for she realized by this inadvertent dropping of his guard, that he had, in fact, been "putting her on" for a long time. She began to give him more advanced and challenging work, and adopted a sterner manner. Evan, realizing that his bluff had lost its effec-

129

tiveness, began reluctantly to give her about a fifty-per-cent effort.

If Evan only partially concealed his abilities at therapy, he concealed them totally at nursery school. He spoke very little there and when he did, it was with only one word. As far as I could gather, he did not participate in learning activities with the group at all. I knew that the papers and projects brought home were not done by him. The teachers were extremely kind to him, however, and more or less allowed him to move about the room on his own, rather than forcing behavioral conformity on him. Whether this was desirable or not is an open question, but I believe it was probably the only possible recourse at that time. The center now had a special nursery school for aphasic children and Evan was first on the waiting list. He would definitely start in June, and I eagerly looked forward to what the experience might do for him.

Until that day when Dr. Ward could see what I was seeing in Evan and make the judgment I hoped for, I could not allow myself a feeling of anything like success. Was I doing enough? I did not believe that because Evan was doing some kindergarten and early first-grade work he was, therefore, two years ahead of himself. I only hoped that his advancement in some areas could provide the needed balance for his slowness in others. He might know his numbers and letters but he lacked much—oh, so much—of the general knowledge most three, or even two-year-olds had. He was innocent of even such facts as having grandparents, aunts, uncles and cousins living in different areas of the country. To be sure, he occasionally saw some of these relatives but the concept of family relationship—let alone the idea of the existence of far off cities—required much too sophisticated an explanation for him to begin to grasp. Similarly there was no way of verbally conveying even the simple fact that a voice on the telephone belonged to a certain person living in another house or town. To Evan this instrument was a talking toy much like a music box. Don called from school regularly and spoke to him in order to give him an opportunity to figure it out for himself but we could not be sure if understanding was taking place.

Evan's comprehension of words had increased by at least ninety-five percent, but this would not have been apparent to the casual observer. Ordinary conversation was still almost entirely beyond him, but I was confident that, with time, his growing recognition of words would begin to give that "hum" more meaning.

Our lessons were still modeled on my original idea; that is, to teach Evan all that he could learn. It was almost coincidental that I found out that what he could comprehend well enough to learn was almost entirely scholastic. So he could not learn now that Grandmother lived in a city thousands of miles away but could talk to him on the telephone. Very well; he could learn all this later when his auditory comprehension had improved. We would spend our time now concentrating on the classroom skills and concepts which were within his reach.

Our work with letters had raised the question once again of Evan's visual perception. His original apparent inability to interpret pictures had led me to assume that his perception was probably impaired. When he had, rather suddenly, found the ability to "see" pictures, and even more significantly to learn to recognize shapes without difficulty, I wondered about it. Had we been mistaken about the probability of impairment? Or had it indeed been a fact and now had a "new pathway" been formed in the brain? As Evan had gone on to learn numbers and letters with apparent ease, I had ceased thinking of his visual perception as a practical problem. Then as we began to work with some of the letters I had saved until last, I noticed that Evan had some difficulty learning *W*. He confused it with *M*. He had similar trouble with *V*, mistaking it for *A*. These two minor obstacles in alphabet learning seemed significant to me. Did Evan then, have difficulty interpreting the difference between *upside down* and *right side up?* Would learning to read pose a great problem for him, along with everything else, I worried? I had been thinking lately of teaching Evan to read three or four words simply to convey the concept that groups of letters represent units of speech. I decided to do this now with the additional intention of ascertaining just how much difficulty Evan would have in learning words.

When introducing a new subject, three always seemed to be the magic number in conveying the underlying concept. So I chose three words which Evan had known for a long time, "car," "ball," and his own name "Evan." I carefully printed each of these words on a separate square of paper making flash cards of them. Bringing out the little cards at the conclusion of the pre-reading segment of Evan's lesson, I held each card up for him to see, carefully enunciating each word. Then I held up the word "car" again, and repeated it but this time I laid the card upon a toy car I had placed beside the table. In a like manner, I held up the word "ball," pronounced it and placed it upon a large rubber ball. The card "Evan," was balanced upon his head for a few moments. I repeated this procedure three or four times before putting the cards away. This idea of placing the printed words on the objects they represented was not of my own invention. I had read of it somewhere but even at the time could not remember where.

The second day I brought out the cards again; this time asking "What's this?", as I presented each word. Getting no responses, I repeated my performance of the previous day and after going over the words three or four times, again held each card up and asked him to identify it. He had obviously gotten the idea now and he looked closely at the words attempting to distinguish between them. On the third day, when I held the cards up, he knew "car" immediately, so I added the word, "rug" to our collection. By the fourth day, he could identify "Evan" and "ball" and by the fifth, he knew "rug." With each word that he mastered, I introduced a new one: "leg," "bed," and "Mama" were now included in our word group.

When he had gotten up to nine or ten words, which was very soon, I had to stop and quiz myself. Just what was it I was intending to do? My original goal had been realized. Evan definitely understood what a printed word was. Also it was obvious that he was not going to have any great difficulty with reading. Was I going to go on with the words and, in fact, teach him to read? Should I? I knew that some authorities had negative views on parents teaching pre-schoolers to read. I had been dubious over the validity of much of their reasoning on the subject anyway, but at any rate, ours was not a normal situation and the usual criteria for determining how a child should be guided were not always applicable to Evan. If he could get a head start on reading now, why not? There would be plenty of things for him to struggle with once he reached school age. His limited auditory comprehension would, for instance, make even the most elementary history or social studies lesson a Herculean undertaking. If Evan did not have to grapple with basic reading skills, along with comprehension, it would surely be to his advantage. Also the realization that he was *good* at something might be just enough to give him confidence in himself when confronted by some of the hurdles which loomed ahead.

I had made my decision. I *would* teach Evan to read. I would be very careful about it though. It would be a

133

casual, pleasurable pursuit. Under no circumstances must Evan be allowed to feel that this was a high-pressure activity. Probably one of the dangers of preschool reading is that it is a glamour skill. To be able to boast to yourself, if to no one else, that your three- or four-year-old tyke can read is heady wine. Thus, a tendency to push too hard could easily develop.

Teaching Evan to read would not become my primary goal. Reading might well become one of his most valuable tools but it would be useless without comprehension. So in the meantime, there were many other things to learn which were of greater importance.

Actually once Evan understood the concept of reading we needed only three to five minutes of our lesson time to work at this endeavor at first. It was not necessary, after the first five or six words, to place the flash cards upon the objects they represented. It did not take long to run through our small, if growing, collection of words. I pretty much followed the formula of introducing a new word as soon as he was able to identify the most recently given one. But if he took more than the usual two or three days to learn a certain word, I would go ahead and introduce the next anyway. I found that this did not confuse him and he sometimes would learn the newer word soonest. Generally our system worked out to the addition of two or three new words per week. I always gave him all of the words daily no matter how certain he was of some of the older ones. My idea was not only to make sure he did not forget any of them but as in our earlier verbal vocabulary lessons, to almost *engrave* these words upon his brain; to make his recognition of them effortless and automatic.

I took great pains in choosing the words I taught Evan as we went along. The first six or seven words were nouns which were very familiar to him. Then I introduced a verb which he also understood well—"run."

The next three words were nouns and then I gave him one of the adjectives we had worked with verbally—"big." I would go on in this way giving him mostly nouns but about every three words introducing a verb or adjective.

Later on, after Evan had learned eighteen to twenty words, I taught him to read a word he did not understand—"is." This was one of those words which, though used constantly, had not entered Evan's awareness. If one said to him, "The house is big," one might just as well have said "house—big" for these were the only two words he "tuned in" to. He had learned to understand "house" and "big" and when he recognized them, he used deductive reasoning to make some sort of sense of the two words used together. Words like "he" and "is" were to him only unnoticed slurs between meaningful units of speech. I realized that reading could provide an invaluable means of bringing such words to his attention. I could not teach him the meaning of the words but if he became aware of the existence of such a word and could see it, then perhaps he would begin to "hear" it, and absorb some understanding of the way in which it was used. Thereafter, about every tenth or fifteenth word I gave Evan was one of these common but vague words—"is," "the," "have," etc. Having a method of impressing these words upon Evan would alone have made the reading lessons worthwhile.

I was careful to space the teaching of words similar in appearance. Thus I did not introduce two new words beginning with the same letter during a week or ten day period. Also, and this was a departure from most primers I have seen, I separated the teaching of words opposite in meaning. If "big" was Evan's tenth word, then "little" might be his thirtieth. I found that he could easily confuse such words, perhaps because he had learned to comprehend their meanings at the same time.

In April 1969, however, we were just beginning our reading lessons. We were working on something else too, of such great importance that I now realized I should have taught this as one of our earliest lessons. That was parts of the body. Besides teaching Evan his "ears," "eyes," "nose" and "mouth," I had made a point during his baths of naming other parts of his body as I washed them. But one evening a friend who was visiting us took Evan upon his knee and began to converse with him.

"What's that?"

"Ears."

"What's that?"

"Nose."

When our friend came to the forehead, cheeks and chin, leaving Evan at a loss for answers, I knew immediately what the next day's vocabulary lesson would involve. A four-year-old should know what to call the various parts of his own body. I should have realized that it would be necessary to teach them to Evan in the form of an academic lesson. Such memorization took concentration, and our sessions were the only period in which he was conditioned to concentrate with adequate intensity.

Towards the conclusion of the next day's lesson, I seated Evan upon our work table in front of me so that I could easily touch him. Beginning with the four sense organs he already knew, I touched each of these in turn, asking "What's this?" When Evan had made the appropriate responses, I went on to his hair, giving it a gentle tug. To my own surprise he did not know this as "hair" but as "comb-your-hair." Once again I realized how terrifically difficult it is for the aphasic child to "pick up" even those vocabulary words which he hears over and over. If I were to help Evan I must constantly be on my guard never to assume his comprehension. "Hair" and "neck" were the two words we worked with that day and then we went on to "arm" and "leg," which he already knew. We played this touch-and-name word game daily, gradually adding parts of the body to our list. Evan learned these body terms more rapidly than he had ever learned anything, and certainly with more interest. I realized that this was more than an important vocabulary accomplishment. Psychological gains involving concepts of self and body-image were being made.

One afternoon Evan interrupted our drill. I had just touched his leg and he had identified it, and I now had my hand on his foot. "What's this?" Moving my hand back to his leg, he looked at me and said, *"Evan! Leg. Evan!"* His eyes were oddly agitated as they searched mine. He had something important to tell me. Could he make me understand? He slapped his leg and exclaimed again, *"Evan! Leg. Evan!"* It had suddenly occurred to him, he was telling me, that this leg was something in and of itself, and yet part of that whole self called "Evan."

"Yes! That's *right,* Evan," I confirmed, giving the leg an emphatic pat. "Leg—Evan. The *leg* is part of *Evan!* It's a *leg* and it's *Evan* too. Yes! Leg—Evan." His features relaxed into a pleased smile as he realized that he had successfully conveyed his thoughts. He had never attempted to express such an independent conceptual observation before. But then, we had never come so close to "discussing" that subject each human being finds of such overwhelming interest—self, *I am.* I had been reaching in, prodding his intellect to perceive what I could offer. But now—now he was reaching out, seeking to tell me of other revelations that were taking place inside. It was what I had been waiting for!

**E**van's mastery of the names of his body parts and the inner speculation and self-awareness which apparently resulted from it brought him noticeably forward in maturity. He had a certain new confidence and self-assurance which he had not had before. He did not hover quite so close to me as he had and, for the first time he conceded to making some effort toward dressing himself.

After teaching Evan all of his main physical accoutrements, I went on to teach him parts of *parts,* expecting some confusion to arise. This was not the case. He already knew that his legs included individual curiosities which needed names—"knees," "ankles"—just as his head had a term of its own, but contained many other entities with names of their own. Although Evan's instinctive self-knowlege made these lessons easy, I did use my customary rule in teaching him: *never teach like, similar or related things at the same time.* Thus I did not teach him "hair" and "head" together, nor "leg" and "knee" nor even "elbow" and "knee."

Evan was due for his April pediatric checkup. I was looking forward to telling the doctor of Evan's progress. Should I tell him about the reading, I wondered? Perhaps the doctor would disapprove. I had already made up my mind about the desirability of teaching Evan this skill, and I did not feel like justifying it to anyone. It was not easy to make such decisions but I knew that I was the only person who understood Evan's intellectual abilities well enough to decide. Lord knew the doctor did not have any suggestions for offering Evan adequate mental stimulation. Maybe I would wait and tell him our secret on the next three-month visit. By then Evan should have learned a substantial number of words and there would be no argument as to whether or not he was ready for such work.

My timing in arranging this appointment was far from ideal. Just the week before we had been through one of those minor ordeals only parents of children unable to communicate can appreciate. Evan had awakened, crying, around ten-thirty one evening, and Don and I had been unable to comfort him. Evan had never yet made any effort to verbally express his fears or pain. He did not understand, or at least did not respond to questions like "What's the matter?" or "What's wrong?" At length we concluded that these were not wails of fear, therefore he must be in pain. There were no signs of illness at all, no clues as to the source of the trouble. As Don paced the floor debating whether or not he should call the doctor. I attempted to reach Evan with the limited communication we had established. Questions were no good. I knew he could not answer them but I was certain he understood the word "hurt."

"Does Evan *hurt?* Evan *hurt—hurt?"* I repeated the word, giving him a chance to connect it to the pain he seemed to be feeling. *"Show* Mama the *hurt. Touch* the *hurt."* Over and over I repeated these words, trying to make him understand. "Evan! Put your finger on the *hurt."* I took his forefinger. *"Touch* the hurt."

Finally he opened his mouth and aimed his finger in the general direction of his throat. With some difficulty I examined it, but could see neither inflammation nor signs of abnormality.

"He pointed to his throat," I told Don, "but it isn't red or anything. You don't think he might have swallowed a chicken bone, do you?"

We had had chicken for dinner and since Evan nad no visible cold symptoms, an ordinary sore throat seemed unlikely. Don and I looked at each other, wordlessly

140

making our decision. We would have to call the doctor. Our suspicions could easily be illfounded under the circumstances, but we'd have to take the chance.

The pediatrician who was on call that evening was not the one we usually saw but he was very understanding and agreed that he should take a look at Evan. By the time we met him in the hospital emergency ward, it was close to midnight, and as so often happens in these situations, Evan had almost completely quieted down. Relieved, feeling a bit foolish, but still not completely discounting our fears, we told the doctor of the evening's events as he checked Evan over. No symptoms of illness, he agreed. Yes, there was still the possibility of a foreign object lodged in the throat tissue. The discomfort from such a thing could sometimes subside for a while. He would order some X-rays.

Evan, already apprehensive about being in this large, strange place in the middle of the night, was terrified by the X-ray apparatus. It took all the strength Don had to hold him still long enough for the technician to take his pictures. When the pediatrician examined the films, he could find nothing. So, our minds reasonably at ease, Don and I bundled up our little boy and took him home anxious to forget the entire experience. The mystery, I believe, was solved a few weeks later. Although Evan was perfectly well the day following the hospital incident, he began to develop conjunctivitis in his right eye on the day after that. I called the pediatrician immediately and with the medication he prescribed, the infection had almost disappeared in a matter of hours, nipped in the bud. Two weeks later I woke up with a terrific eye infection which my ophthalmologist treated. Like Evan, I had no other symptoms of any general illness, but two days after that I had a sharp and continuous pain deep in my throat for the better part of the day. I realized then that

141

this must have been what Evan was experiencing that night, and that it was, apparently, connected in some way with the conjunctivitis.

Evan's routine pediatric checkup had already been scheduled for the week following the hospital experience. Once we were in the office I wished I had postponed it. His fear of the X-ray instruments still fresh in his mind, Evan refused to stand on the scale for the nurse or even for me. When our pediatrician came to the examination room, he took Evan into the hall and managed to weigh him himself. Unnerved from the start at this insistence upon his standing on the scale, Evan cried and reacted fearfully to all the doctor's instruments in a way he had not done in almost a year. Disappointed that the pediatrician could not be seeing Evan at his best, I explained about the trauma at the hospital and that this was obviously the cause of the trouble now. I went on to give him a brief account of the progress Evan had been making; the concepts he had learned, his extensive advancement in word comprehension, his ability to identify numbers and letters, and—impulsively, I reversed my former decision—the fact that he had even learned to read a few words.

The doctor listened impassively, apparently unimpressed with (or, possibly, skeptical of) my words. As he finished his examination, he sent Evan back to me to be dressed and asked me a few questions about Evan's therapy and schooling. Then, apropos of nothing in particular, he casually remarked, "Well, *I* think he's mentally retarded."

"But—but—why?" I gasped, hardly believing I had heard him correctly. Only nine months before we had sat in this very room as he told me that he believed as I did, that Evan was of normal intelligence.

"Because he's so emotionally upset," the pediatrician began in the manner of a teacher who enjoys explaining

142

the logic behind a theory. "You see, a child would not be so upset in this situation unless he were: one, emotionally disturbed; two, mentally retarded; or three, a combination of the two. Now we know that Evan's trouble cannot be solely emotional disturbance. There would be no reason for it. After all you don't beat him. Therefore it must be mental retardation, or at least, partly that and partly emotional disturbance. Do you see?" he concluded, almost brightly.

I blinked stupidly, speechless for a moment at the rapidity and confidence with which he had reached such a shattering conclusion. After all how did he know I didn't mistreat the child? For all the man knew, I locked Evan in closets all day.

Finding my voice I argued, "But he *is* neurologically handicapped and Dr. Ward told us that a child as severely handicapped as Evan *will* have emotional problems."

"Well, but—neurologically handicapped. . . ." The pediatrician shrugged, giving me a meaningful look.

Receiving his message I protested, "But neurologically handicapped isn't the same thing as mentally retarded! Is it?"

The doctor simply nodded, slowly, sympathetically but with deliberate finality. "I'm telling you this now," he explained, "so that you will realize his limitations, and not push him toward goals he can never attain. If you lead him to expect to be able to perform on a normal level with his peers, he will become terribly frustrated when he finds he cannot and severe emotional disturbance will result. So don't push him. Just try to make him as happy as possible at his own level."

This was good advice for parents of a retarded child; I *knew* it was good advice. Yet if, as the doctor claimed, Evan was mentally retarded, why didn't the admonition seem applicable?

Because, I thought later in the car, because Evan had not been at *all* happy left at his "own level." On the contrary, he had become noticeably happier and more confident as he had developed new abilities. Could it possibly be wrong to teach him when he seemed so eager and able to learn? Was I, as the doctor had hinted, giving Evan false hopes? *Happy. Happy* was the key word. It was what the doctor had been talking about, and it was really the only thing I was concerned with. Achingly aware of the little boy in the back seat, who loved and trusted me completely, I knew with complete certainty that my aspirations for him were unadulterated by any selfish motives. I was not motivated by feelings that *I* could not have an imperfect child, that *my* child must be as good as anyone's. I knew in my heart that if Evan were truly mentally retarded and could live happily as such, I would be content. But—I knew he could *not* be happy in ignorance. He wanted to learn. Certainly I had found that he was able to learn. He had a fantastic memory and retained almost everything he learned. If he could learn and retain the things his peers were learning, could he still be mentally retarded? Or, if he *were* intellectually deficient but could go on learning at a normal level, what difference would it make? He might never know.

My thoughts were not making any sense at all, I realized. The term, mentally retarded, was beginning to seem meaningless.

Disentangling myself from the confusion my train of thought had led me into, I took a fresh approach to the problem. First of all, was my teaching making Evan unhappy? No, quite the reverse. Although he might not enjoy every single exercise that comprised our lessons, over all he derived pleasure from his new knowledge and abilities. Second question. Was I urging Evan to reach for the unobtainable? The answer, I was sure, was *no* again. I was not comparing Evan to anyone, insisting that he live up to the standards of any group, real or hypothetical. I had begun the lessons with the objective that I would teach him *what he was able to learn*, and I felt I had adhered to that. There had been the color incident, of course, but fortunately my instincts had proven correct. Since then I had proceeded with studied caution. As with the drawing and number concepts, I quietly withdrew specific exercises he did not succeed at, taking care to show neither impatience nor disappointment. I reintroduced the concepts after a period but in a different way to avoid establishing a pattern of repeated failure. The larger portions of our time were spent at the things he was easily progressing in: vocabulary, prereading activities and reading. Here I had found what his own pace was and let him proceed at it.

To sum up then, the lessons were a positive not a negative factor in Evan's life. The only goal I was guiding him toward was the fulfillment of his *own* potential, whatever that might be. Assuming that he *was* mentally retarded, it would still be important for him to fulfill that potential, however limited. I would go on as I had, concerning myself with the practicalities of teaching Evan, trying not to dwell on the worry of how far he could go. Employing the method of self-discipline I had taught myself to use when agonizing over the unanswerable question of Evan's future, I forced my mind upon the ever-constant search for solutions to some of my teaching problems. Drawing was an area in which I hadn't come up with anything new lately. I needed to try something completely new. Paper and crayons did not interest Evan at all. How about a blackboard and chalk? I had been thinking I should try this for some time but now I concentrated my mental energies upon the idea as if it were the most urgent issue facing me. Turning into the driveway I noted with sinking heart the empty garage. It was only four-thirty. Don was not home yet. The

145

girls' bicycles were gone; they would still be at play. I could *not* stay in the silent house, easy prey to the thoughts I wished to avoid. Putting the car into reverse, I backed into the street again and headed toward a nearby department store.

Vainly I searched through the toy section unable to find the type of blackboard I was looking for. I would have to wait until I could get to a larger store. Still I could not go home empty-handed. I felt a desperate need to take something with me that promised potential progress—a symbol, I suppose, of hope. Finally I settled on two new story books which I would "rewrite" and a simple coloring book.

This time when Evan and I arrived home Don was already there. Showing him my purchases, I began to babble of our pressing need for a blackboard.

"What did the doctor say?" asked Don when we had settled the question of where and when we would get the needed toy.

"Well," I began, "in the first place, Evan behaved terribly. He was frightened and upset from his experience at the hospital last week." I went on to describe the incident with the scale and Evan's behavior during the examination. Finally, feeling that I had given him some idea of the situation, I told Don of the doctor's words. He had been waiting for bad news. From the moment I had walked in the door he could tell, by what he later described as the "glazed" expression in my eyes, that something was very wrong.

Indignantly we began to discredit the doctor's opinion. We discussed the shaky evidence he had based his conclusion on. It had not been a fair test. Evan had been frightened. Any child could become frightened in such a situation but most particularly a child who could not understand soothing explanations of what was going on. The doctor certainly could not make a valid judgment on Evan under these unusual circumstances. Our arguments were logical, we both genuinely realized that they were, and yet. . . .

The damaging fact was that a man, because he bore a title had, whether we respected his opinion or not, put a label on Evan. We had to take a gamble and see if we could lift that damning label before it left a mark. We would take Evan back to Children's Hospital for a psychological re-evaluation. He had made such strides in the past year. Perhaps Dr. Ward could now ascertain that Evan was of normal intelligence. We knew, too, that we had to face the possibility that the psychologist would agree with our doctor. I had not really felt yet that Evan was ready to be re-tested. I had wanted to bring him a little further in our lessons and I certainly had wanted to wait until he was responding to his therapist in a more satisfactory manner. If Evan did pass the test, we could erase the pediatrician's words from our minds forever. If Evan failed to pass it, little would be changed. We would still believe that he had simply not passed it *yet*. If Dr. Ward concurred with our pediatrician to the extent that he now definitely felt that Evan was mentally retarded, it would be discouraging indeed, but we were not prepared to give up. In that case we would assume that Evan had given Dr. Ward the same performance he gave his therapist and teachers and go on as we had been—waiting and hoping.

During the week preceding our second visit to Dr. Ward, Don and I endeavored to prepare ourselves for the failure we so feared we would meet. Again and again we reminded each other of the convincing way in which Evan feigned ignorance in his therapy sessions. He would surely do the same thing for Dr. Ward. We just really could not expect to get any kind of valid evaluation. No, someday Evan would allow others to see him as we did but it was too soon now, too soon. This was only a casual, annual check with Dr. Ward to see if, by some extremely remote chance, he could determine anything positive at such an early date. In all probability it would be at least another year before Evan could understand and cooperate sufficiently to be tested at all accurately. We, of course, would be seeing Dr. Ward at this time next year. This year's test was of no special importance. So we comforted ourselves in preparation for the disappointment we expected.

At Don's request Sister Elizabeth called me at home and provided me with the kind of moral support I so needed at that point. She was in a somewhat difficult position, since she did not care to compromise her professional ethics by criticizing our doctor. She managed, nonetheless, to emphatically get across one important message: she did *not* believe Evan to be mentally retarded. As she talked to me, my shakened confidence reasserted itself. The Sister well understood her role in the lives of parents who, but for her, would have stood alone in their faith. It could not have been a comfortable role for she assumed the risk of being wrong. She would not have had to have shared this burden of possible error but she knew how much it meant to us to have just one qualified person express our own beliefs. I sensed that Sister Elizabeth was haunted by the same

149

thought as I: tragic though it might be to hold the belief that a child has normal intelligence and later be proven in error, how much more tragic to accept prematurely a limited potential and thus doom a possibly intelligent child to a lifetime imprisonment within himself.

By the time we presented ourselves at the hospital on a rather gloomy spring morning, Don and I felt we had achieved the proper frame of mind. We did not expect good news but we would not regard the outcome as bad news either, but rather, as no news at all. Evan was due at his regular therapy session later in the morning. We would go as usual, have lunch somewhere and perhaps do some shopping. It would just be a day, not *quite* like any other, but not of any special significance either.

When Dr. Ward appeared, Don simply told him that we felt that Evan had made a great deal of progress over the past year and we were just wondering if he would be able to see it too. Evan trustingly took the psychologist's hand and followed him slowly down the corridor leaving Don and me to thumb nervously through magazines.

"I hope he gives him a lot of puzzles," muttered Don once, and I smiled in appreciation. Evan was good at puzzles. Trying to ignore my psychosomatic stomach which was feeling a bit uneasy, I tried arduously to interest myself in the tribulations of a bosomy actress who resented being considered a sex symbol. Giving up, I laid the magazine aside and allowed myself to pessimistically envision the performance Evan no doubt was putting on. As I checked my watch for what must have been the eighteenth time, Evan suddenly reappeared in the waiting room. Dr Ward was following close behind, and he was smiling! It was the kind of smile that told us immediately that what we had hardly dared to hope for had happened!

"It's really remarkable," he declared in answer to our

150

eager questions. "He has progressed at least—at *least* —eighteen months in the past year. In many of the tests he actually performed at a normal four-year-old level. His intellect, that is, his *inner potential*, is definitely unimpaired. Of course, his aphasia *is*, as I first told you, extremely severe. His vocabulary, though, is pretty much on a four-year-old plane. I know that sounds contradictory—do you know what I mean?"

I nodded my comprehension. The fact that Evan could understand so little ordinary conversation and yet had now attained an almost normal knowledge of vocabulary words did not seem paradoxical to me. I had groped my way through the pathways of Evan's brain and understood the connections yet to be made.

"You know," the psychologist continued, "He has no hostility whatever, which is amazing. Usually a child of this age with so great a handicap is very distrustful. Of course, Evan almost certainly will have some emotional problems."

Again I nodded as did Don. Some of Evan's behavior for a long time probably would come under the heading of *emotional problems.* There had been the tantrums, and of course Evan's behavior at school and with his therapist was—well—*peculiar.*

"Now, you do realize," Dr. Ward warned as if out of reluctant duty, "that even though Evan certainly possesses a normal *intellectual* potential, he can become retarded through the severity of his handicap."

"Yes, I know. I know he could, but he won't. I just *know* he won't now!" I exclaimed, happily. "I've always known that if the potential were there, he would make it. I was *sure* it was, but now—now we *know!*"

Don and I fairly bounded down the hospital steps with Evan. It was official! It was on record that Evan was of normal intelligence! No longer would we have to tell ourselves why and how *we* knew this to be so. It *was* so. We were freed forever from the slightest possible doubt. Never again could our confidence be undermined by anyone's poorly considered opinion. No more would I have to remind myself as I taught Evan that I just might be working with an impaired intellect. And the wheels of that intellect were turning—operating at a more than normal rate.

". . . Progressed at *least* eighteen months in the past year . . . normal four-year-old level in many of the tests . . ." He was catching up, making up for lost time! The channel I had carved through to that inner child had indeed reached him. We would chip away at the walls of that channel, making it wider and wider until Evan himself could step through. Then he would take his place with his peers—talking with them—laughing with them, comparing strengths and weaknesses. Perhaps he would always have some problem with speech but he might be a star algebra student—why not? Or the most valuable player on the football team. He might possess a handicap, but it would definitely not possess him. A severely handicapped child who could accomplish in twelve months what a normal child did in eighteen could do almost anything he desired if he tried hard enough.

It was still too early for Evan's therapy session and we drove to a dingy little coffee shop. Sipping at cups of coffee, Don and I happily anticipated the phone calls we would make as soon as we got home. We would call my parents and Don's mother, of course, and let's see, the Madsens would want to know and Barbara and Jim, and. . . ." We babbled on as we fondly watched Evan gobble down an enormous doughnut and a Coke. His eyes sparkled as he surveyed his surroundings. This was his kind of treat! He grinned at us as he swallowed the last morsel of doughnut and indulgently we ordered him

152

another. We would not behave sensibly today! We would have lunch at his favorite restaurant, go shopping—perhaps buy him a new toy—do those things which to him were great adventures. Tomorrow, Evan and I would be hard at work on our lessons, again. But not today. Today was for celebrating!

Everything seemed to have changed. We were happy as we had not been in a year, for we were now firmly confident that we were on the right road. Yet I was uneasy about my tutoring sessions. Just as we were experiencing this joyously dramatic turning point in our lives, Evan's lessons began to assume a different shape. Whereas from the start *concepts* and *vocabulary* had been our most vital areas of endeavor with reading activities, drawing and numbers taking secondary importance as outgrowths of concept work, this situation now seemed to be reversing itself. Evan was making his greatest progress in reading accomplishments. He had mastered his letters, he was learning to read double-digit numbers, he knew every shape and symbol I had been able to think of, and of course he was steadily increasing his knowledge of words. With renewed vigor, now that I had a professional confirmation of Evan's intellectual competence, I was broadening my attack on number concepts. Drawing was, for the time being, still only a sometime thing, but I was beginning to concentrate more of my energies on devising new ways of interesting him in this. *Vocabulary* and *concepts* were something we worked on at the end of our lessons, usually in combined form—the word and the concept, more often than not, being the same thing. The words "happy," "sad," "afraid" and "mad," for example, had to be demonstrated by exaggerated expressions and actions in order to convey the idea of the various emotions. There was not the rapid advancement in these areas as before, particularly from the standpoint of vocabulary learning. We worked with only a fraction of the number of words we had formerly worked with. In short our lessons now seemed to consist of the *Three R's, plus.*

What was I doing, I worried? Was I getting off course,

carried away by the psychologist's report? The fact of Evan's severe aphasia had not been altered. Speech comprehension and the learning of the concepts which normally required language to establish were still his main problems. Surely I was not forgetting this! Why change the direction of our lessons now when it had just been so gratifyingly proven that I was on the right track? Yet upon reflection I realized that the change had begun to take place even before we had seen Dr. Ward. It had been a natural occurrence, not a change of direction but rather the passing of a milestone on our way.

I was too close to the mechanics of my strivings to be able to understand in perspective the full significance of this progression to more conventional scholastic pursuits. For six months Evan and I had worked—rapidly but unrecognizingly passing through two learning subphases which comprised one basic, elementary phase. We were now passing into the second phase and a more or less permanent educational form. All fall and winter we had, in actuality, been laying a *foundation* for learning in Evan's mind. Just as he could now slowly build his language comprehension upon all the vocabulary words he had learned, so he could structure his education on the basic concepts he possessed. He was now—in a word —educable, whereas, before he had not been.

As for finding the "key" to communication of which Dr. Ward had spoken, I suppose I always had that. Like most mothers I could speak to my child without words and when I encountered difficulties in this, I instinctively knew what methods to try in getting through to him. Now, however, his comprehension of separate ordinary words, and his knowledge of basic concepts provided others with a key to teaching and communicating with him, granted they were educated in using it.

Going back to my own analogy of a *foundation,* I found our lessons undergoing a marked transformation because I had now finished laying that foundation. As Dr. Ward had mentioned, Evan's *word* vocabulary was almost on a normal four-year-old level. There were no more large groups of important words to systematically pour into his mind. Now it would be a matter of keeping on my toes to see that he learned the names of new things as he was exposed to them, and most of all, to build on that secure foundation of words by using them in conversation and in conjunction with other less demonstrable words. His reading, both listening and learning, would also help to form the structure of language. With the words that he understood, it was now possible to carry on this building throughout each day, but most of all, during our lessons, in which each learning activity was also an exercise in language usage. Besides this, I began to carry on certain carefully structured conversations with Evan at the end of each lesson to convey usage of certain words. "You," "I" and "me," for example, were words he would only come to understand through constant repetition in conjunction with words and ideas he already knew. These words are terribly confusing, because their meanings change every time a different person uses them. Thus I would ask, "What are *you* wearing?" pointing to him in the beginning. I had previously taught him "wear" and "wearing" with the use of paper dolls—"What is the Mama wearing?"

Evan might reply, "You wearing blue shirt?"

"No, Evan, say *I* am wearing a blue shirt. *I* . . . *I* am w . . ." I would correct him, pointing to his shirt. Then I would ask, "What am *I* wearing?"

"Pink dress?"

"*Who* is wearing a pink dress?" This was a good exercise for learning "who," also.

This sort of conversation could take place daily for several weeks before I felt he was truly beginning to understand the two or three new words involved. Certainly the advances were not as dramatic as in our earlier foundation vocabulary word, but this structural building took longer. Much of our *concept* work was also included in this structured conversation period.

"What do you *see?*" I would ask, at first pointing suggestively to objects.

"What do you *hear?*"I would ask next, knocking loudly on the wall or singing or whistling.

From time to time I still tested him on already learned concepts making sure that he did not lose these. Also I still worked with the many many words for different spatial positions, for I did not think he was yet totally secure in his knowledge of those. Although he almost always answered my questions on positions correctly, his voice was hesitant, lacking that triumphant certainty so typical of his usual recitations.

The new and more conventional structure of our lessons now made it much easier for me to plan and organize material for Evan to learn. *Reading, writing, arithmetic* and *general knowledge,* I would think to myself finding it convenient to fit our activities into these four categories. These lofty terms—while sounding rather silly and presumptuous considering our achievement level—guided my planning, for they kept me in mind of the direction our activities were aimed in. The things we were doing now were the beginnings of the subjects Evan would be studying for a long time. I knew what he would eventually be expected to accomplish in these subjects—or would if he were not handicapped. It was the closest I had come to having a prelaid plan. Evan was actually preparing for his formal education. If I could give him a headstart in this, make him secure in the basic concepts and familiar with the general precepts which comprised each subject, then he should be equipped to get a fairly normal education in spite of his handicap.

And so I continued my work with Evan in the subjects

with the impressive names, but with a new self-assurance and certainty of goal. *Reading,* which he enjoyed the most, meant letters, number reading, word cards, and reviews of shapes and symbols. *Writing* meant drawing and pre-writing exercises, although this was still an on-again, off-again endeavor. *Arithmetic* at this time simply meant different exercises aimed at instilling the quantitative number concept and counting. *General knowledge* included anything I felt Evan ought to be familiar with. Conversation, new words; old and new verbal concepts were assigned to this category and also anything else I felt that a child his age should have knowledge of. This was where I would begin systematic usage of my "familiarization" notion. Using all of the language we had established plus any visual aids I could make or find, I would concentrate on giving Evan a sketchy knowledge or simply an awareness of things, from calendars and money to addresses and phone numbers of personages, from President Nixon to Peter Rabbit. By this I hoped to remove a little of the mystery from Evan's world. I wanted to get him to the place where ordinary conversation would, rather than draw a complete blank, produce a response equivalent to, "Hmm—I don't understand, but I *am* familiar with what you are talking about." It would be a bridge and if Evan could cross over to the bewildering land of people with language, I knew he could find a place with them.

I knew now that that inner child was whole and undamaged and that my efforts were enabling him to grow at a more than satisfactory pace. I could not, however, lead him into that outer world, for I was not a part of it. He must take the hand of someone else. I could only continue to strengthen his capabilities until he felt confident enough to do this.

Although, as Dr. Ward had told us, Evan was able to perform at a completely normal level in many areas, he was careful to hide his ability from others. It was discouraging to see his hard-won knowledge going unused in his outside contacts. Whatever his emotional attitude was—and it was perplexing even to me—I knew it was not going to be easy to change. Someone, some outsider, must convey to Evan that he was *adequate*. Yet, how could this possibly come to happen if he gave no hint of his adequacy? He offered nothing to confirm.

At just over four years, Evan's demeanor at school was that of a child under two. Although there were some things he could have done as well as his peers, he refused to try, feigning ignorance. His behavior with his therapist had improved somewhat but he still kept his attitude and performance months behind that of home. At home it was more difficult to describe his behavior in terms of age. Generally, I suppose, it was two-and-one-half to three, but when he was involved in some mental activity, as in our lessons, he was much like a four-year-old foreign child who did not understand the language very well.

We were not concerned about Evan's immature behavior at home. The important fact was that he *was* making steady and gratifying progress there. The tantrums had declined to a minimum. He was using, more and more, the speech he had learned in our lessons. He had always

161

been super-secure with our family, and now that he realized he was growing within it and was more able to communicate with us, he seemed almost completely happy. The outside world was bewildering and perhaps seemingly hostile, but this safe inner world of family was all the world that Evan seemed to want. He enjoyed our friends and those of his sisters, who visited our home, for they were part of that world too. He was friendly and unselfconscious when he went places so long as a member of the family accompanied him. This was because we were his only world and, as the much-loved little one, he was not expected to move independently outside of it. Evan did not wish to grow up and lose his right to the protection given a family baby. He was not ready to meet the world all alone. Thus, although he was obviously happy to be able to relate to us on a more mature and meaningful level, he was careful to secure his dependent role by deliberately clinging to certain baby habits. Two glaring examples of these infantile ways were his insistence upon eating most of his meals with his fingers and his refusal to toilet train—most particularly the latter. Unfortunately, society places an inordinate amount of emphasis upon this one aspect of maturation and indeed tends to use it as a measure of a child's intelligence. It is not easy for parents to withstand the pressures from outside, and put the matter in the position of importance it deserves. I had known, with almost complete certainty, that Evan had been quite capable of toilet training since, probably, he reached the average age for this. It was not a question of lack of control or comprehension. It was an obvious way of remaining Mama's baby. Knowing that he possessed the capability, I could have made a great issue of toileting, perhaps broken down Evan's defenses and even succeeded in training him; and thereby, in all probability, lost the invaluable rapport I had with him. It was simply not worth it. Toilet training was of such small immediate importance compared with the urgency of freeing his intellect from the nearly drowning bog it had been mired in. The matter belonged in the category of emotional development and this must necessarily proceed more slowly than the intellectual. Evan did not have enough confidence yet to loosen his hold on me. The only thing that bothered me was the fact that I knew it upset our relatives and was a subject of scandal with neighborhood children. However I closed my eyes to all of this as much as possible, confident that all would take place in its own time. Every five or six months I would try for about a week to encourage Evan to use the toilet, potty, coffee can, whatever, but when he steadfastly refused, I would drop the issue again.

As for Evan's eating habits, part of this was refusal to accept mature responsibility, but also, I was certain, inefficient motor control played at least some small part. After Evan's second test Dr. Ward had mentioned probable motor impairment again, and I was beginning to see more evidence of it now. It had been difficult at first because Evan's overall coordination had seemed at least as good as the average. What we had been seeing, of course, was his *gross* motor control. The less obvious *fine* motor coordination was where Evan seemed to have difficulty. I had seen evidence of impaired control in our drawing endeavors as well as in eating habits.

I have been speaking of Evan's demeanor mostly in terms of behavioral age, which is, at best, an incomplete picture. It says little of what Evan was actually *like*. The truth is he was utterly charming. There is something very special about these little children with communication handicaps, at least those who have been cherished. They possess a quality of enchanting purity, for they are uncorrupted by the small mean thoughts which, along with the good, are inculcated by language. Evan's innocence was a protection as well as a compensation, for when he became a target for teasing by neighborhood children, he not only failed to comprehend the childishly cruel jibes, he failed to recognize the unkind motives which prompted them. Unaccustomed as he was to anything but loving treatment, the derisive teasing generally passed over his head.

When he was at play outside, I carefully watched him, biting my nails behind a curtain, or I had Cindy or Wendy reading or playing with him in the yard. At the first sign of real trouble he was casually taken inside or to the fenced-in back yard. Still there were a few painful incidents, but we took comfort in the fact that they probably hurt us more than Evan. He almost never played with other children, but this seemed to be more Evan's fault than that of the other children. Occasionally another small child would wander over and attempt to play with him but Evan, although seemingly somewhat pleased to have another child in the vicinity, would not respond in any way to the other child's overtures. He simply did not seem to know how to relate to other children. From all I could see at nursery school, he did not do much better there although he had been associating with many of the children for two years.

With the family, Evan loved to tease; sharing unexpressed jokes with us, a roguish sparkle in his eyes. When Don would sprawl on the floor, as was his habit, with a book or newspaper spread before him, Evan would stroll casually over and sit on it, mischievously ignoring his Daddy's amused requests to remove himself. He was likely to run off with something necessary to some project one of his sisters might be working on, shrieking with glee as he was pursued. Since I was the teacher of speech, he often took perverse pleasure in deliberately using the wrong word for something, then smiling at my earnest efforts to correct him, saying with his eyes, "Hey, come on Mom, this is all in fun."

164

He was full of affection for each and every member of his family, giving love as easily as he accepted it. And how we all loved him. We knew, as he did, that it was enough for now. *We* were painfully aware, however, that we must prepare him for the time when it would *not* be enough.

Evan's therapist, due to a personal crisis, had left the center very suddenly. Sister Elizabeth was left with the problem of replacing her at once, a job made more difficult because she could not offer anyone a permanent position. Evan's therapist had been planning to leave in the fall and the Sister had already hired a therapist to assume the position at this date. Now she had to find substitutes to fill in the three- or four-month interval. Far from being disturbed at the change, I was eager to see someone else "take a crack at" Evan in a one-to-one situation. His progress with his former therapist had continued to fall far short of what I had hoped for. My goal for now was not even to see Evan learn anything new from a therapist; only to have him perform and recite previously learned skills at the level of his true ability. In other words to "drop his act."

He was to have one substitute therapist for a very few weeks and then another for the three months during the summer. The first of these was Nancy. She was quite attractive, probably about thirty and had a certain look about her that I liked immediately. One would never have guessed she was only filling a position for a few weeks. She had the efficient air of a person who intended to accomplish something. Before her first therapy session with Evan I attempted, in the two or three minutes we had, to acquaint her with what I now considered his greatest problem: the gap between his demeanor and his ability. I hardly expected her to believe me but I was determined to persevere until I found someone who did, even if I did earn myself the reputation of a neurotic

165

screwball. As I watched the first ten minutes of the therapy session through the observation window, Nancy attempted some of the simplest conceptual exercises on Evan without the slightest success. Evan stared vacuously about the room as if he had no knowledge of what she was doing or talking about. Retracing my steps to the waiting room, I took out my pocket notebook and began to write a résumé of Evan's achievements. I enumerated the concepts he was familiar with, made as accurate an evaluation as possible of the level of his language comprehension and wrote of the work he was doing at home. I also elaborated on the problem of his very convincing, helpless demeanor and suggested that Nancy let him know she was not misled by it. At the conclusion of the session, I gave her the résumé, and attempting to give the appearance of complete sanity, I took my apparently incompetent little boy by the hand and led him out.

When I brought Evan to the center for his second session with Nancy, she said nothing to me of what I had written but took Evan directly to the therapy room. Again I watched and again I saw her meet with failure in her attempts to get through to Evan. This time she tried some more difficult games and exercises in addition to the elementary ones, but this apparent effort to stimulate him by offering him a greater challenge proved in vain. Evan either stared blankly at her or ran obliviously back and forth in the little room. Returning dejectedly to the waiting room, I sat down with a disappointed sigh. Nancy would certainly never believe me now. Oh well, another therapist could be coming in a few weeks. Perhaps she would be able to work some magic.

"I would like to talk to you," said Nancy as she returned Evan to my charge. "How would you feel about me getting sort of stern with Evan?"

At once I was all enthusiasm. She realized that what

166

I had said was true! More than that, she was determined to find a way of getting through to Evan.

"Yes," I agreed. "I think that would be a good idea. I am quite firm with him at home when he refuses to perform. I think that by being stern in such a situation, you convey confidence in his ability. Do what your instincts tell you. I'm behind you one hundred percent."

Nancy smiled, pleased with my response. "I always like to have the mother's permission to use sternness. Some parents don't like the idea. I have four children of my own, though, and I have a feeling about when discipline is necessary. As long as you give love too, I think it is beneficial."

I instinctively felt that she knew what she was doing. What she really wanted to do was exactly what I did with Evan. (She was not speaking of *physical punishment* incidentally, but rather, a stricter manner.) I had suggested to his former therapist that she be more firm with Evan but she had seemed reluctant to do this. I had demurred, thinking that perhaps therapists were trained to avoid a disciplinary manner. I, however, like Nancy, felt that just as careful discipline shows a normal child that you love or care about him so it does with a child like Evan. The discipline, to be sure, must be more tempered, more flexible; but insisting (*most* of the time) that he perform at his true level of ability says "I think you're a pretty smart kid!"

At the next session, I watched with hopeful anticipation and some amusement as Nancy put a studied sharpness into her tone at Evan's first refusal to cooperate. She did not put the disdained game away, letting him see that she was giving up, but rather made it abundantly clear by her voice that she was *insisting* that he do it. Finally, almost in spite of himself, Evan complied with her instructions. I could not possibly describe the expression of bewilderment Evan wore throughout the rest

167

of that session as he found himself actually doing a "lesson" almost as he did at home. Nancy praised him and occasionally hugged him when he performed a task successfully. Then, sensitive to the moment when he had had enough, she ceased the mental endeavors and batted a ball back and forth with him.

Nancy was the first outsider to make contact with that intelligent inner child, and thus, was the person who made him take that important initial step toward meeting the world independently. The quality she possessed which made this step possible was, I believe, instinctive. I have seen it with untrained people as well as noticed the lack of it in some who are trained. The quality is based upon an intense *caring,* and somehow conveys the message, "I know you can do this, and you *are* going to do it!"

In the very short time Nancy had with Evan she succeeded in breaking down much of his facade. He began to perform his therapy exercises with a reasonably cooperative attitude. I could see that Evan liked her, probably because he respected her, and although he did not learn anything new from her, he performed previously learned achievements at close to his true capability. By the time Nancy terminated her interim post at the center, she had made him ready for his next therapist.

Evan's therapist for the summer was a young woman named Karen. She was going to begin working toward her master's degree in the fall so the summer job vacancy was a convenient occurrence for her. She sat in on Nancy's last therapy sessions so the changeover for each child could be accomplished as smoothly as possible. I observed as Nancy showed the new therapist how she worked with Evan and explained his particular behavioral problems. She emphasized the fact that he possessed much more ability than he liked to let on to and that firmness was a necessity in dealing with him. I could

168

see that she was giving Karen quite a lengthy evaluation sheet on Evan and I was confident that Karen would begin her work with Evan with full understanding of his abilities and problems.

We could not have been more fortunate in having Karen at this time. Nancy had done her job well in laying the groundwork for Karen to carry on the rapport Nancy herself had established with Evan. If the wrong person had stepped in at this critical time, Evan's recent change of attitude might have reverted before it had a chance to become permanent. One of Karen's greatest advantages in working with Evan was probably her lack of long experience. She certainly knew her job and was proficient in the mechanics of speech therapy, but she had a freshness of attitude, a certain lack of complacence, which allowed her to succeed with Evan where some more experienced therapists might have failed. She was genuinely fond of children and established an affectionate relationship with Evan from the beginning; but even more than that, she *respected* him as a person. To her, Evan was a unique individual. She did not attempt to type him from his behavior patterns, thus fitting him into a convenient category where "I usually work with *these* children *this* way." Rather, she used all the means available to her to find out what made Evan tick and which approach would be most likely to prove successful in each given situation. She was delighted to find out about my own work with Evan and accepted, with never a trace of skepticism, my naturally greater understanding of him.

"Is he really at a loss or is he putting me on?" Karen would ask me when Evan seemed unable to grasp some concept or perform some exercise. When, more often than not, I could tell her that Evan did indeed have knowledge of the activity in question, she could then proceed confidently with a slightly teasing yet firm,

"Come on, Evan, you *know* this." Her somewhat bantering tone seemed exactly right. It conveyed the idea that Evan had only been teasing her, whereas, if she had accepted his attitude as deliberate defiance (which it was), it would have gained impetus.

Karen asked me to let her know of any new concepts I was working on with Evan so that she could reinforce them. Working in close cooperation this way, we managed to provide Evan with maximum benefit from each of our independent endeavors. The most important thing we accomplished was to lift Evan's achievements with me out of the context of "just for Mama." To be sure, he was sharing his knowledge with only one other person besides myself, but this was a significant emotional advancement.

As spring turned into summer my own lessons with Evan were going especially well. We were doing something rather new and exciting (to me) in almost every subject. With the list of words that Evan could read steadily increasing, I had begun to think about the natural eventual goal of all this: reading these words in sentences, in books. I should start guiding him toward an understanding of how one reads words on a page—that is, from left to right, down a line and left again. A page of words, even known words, would be tremendously confusing to him. I would have to ease him into the reading method gradually.

Cutting out long rectangles of paper and using the words Evan already knew, I made a series of flash phrase cards. At first I used phrases of only two or three words, later lengthening some of these to four, five or six words. The phrases or short sentences expressed ideas Evan could readily understand: "I love Evan," "Daddy is big," "Evan is a boy," etc. Using these phrase cards just as I did word cards, I held them up one at a time, pointing to each word as Evan was supposed to read it. He soon caught on to the idea, and it was not too long before I was able to stop pointing to each successive word on the known phrase cards. For quite a while it was necessary to point to each word in new phrases. I found that, unlike the single word cards, these phrase cards should not be learned too well. Memory rote, not to mention perseveration, began to take over at a certain point. For instance, I used the phrase "Evan is a good boy" too often, and when I made a card saying "Evan is a *little* boy," he missed the different word, reciting instead the overlearned phrase. These phrases, then, were to be discarded, changed and rearranged constantly. After all, the point was not to learn the phrases but to form the habit of left to right reading. My purpose also was to deepen his concept of reading itself. He had learned that a printed word symbolized an object, motion or aspect. Now he was learning that a *series* of words expressed an idea or fact. And so, reading period became even more productive as we constantly went over and added to the stack of word cards and Evan began to master sentence reading.

In arithmetic I had finally found an approach that captured Evan's interest. I had been certain for some time now that Evan truly understood the quantitative number concept and was putting me on—what a byword that slang phrase had become in considering Evan's performance at certain times—when he failed to count properly. He had slipped on certain occasions, showing me that he knew what he was doing, and by this time I would have been almost certain anyway. It was definitely that psychological block again. My objective, therefore, was not to instill the concept but to find a way of getting Evan to readily show that he knew it. If I could not succeed in this, I would have no way of helping him develop his number skills. What sort of presentation would possibly appeal to him? Well, which area of learning did he enjoy the most? Reading, no question about that. Reading—of course! Flash cards! He loved the challenge of learning flash cards.

Cutting small paper rectangles just as I had done for his word cards, I imprinted each with varying numbers of different shapes. I made five cards with hearts on them—one heart, two hearts, three hearts, four hearts and five hearts. Likewise, I made five-card groups with squares, stars, circles, rectangles and diamonds. Shuffling the pile of cards, I put them with our word cards. These new cards were at the bottom of the stack when next I ran through our word exercise with Evan. When I came to the first number-concept card, I was careful to behave as if there were nothing unusual about it.

"Star," said Evan, finally, after blinking at it.

"Yes, yes, star," I agreed casually. "But how *many* stars? *Two* stars." I answered my own question before the pause could become too "pregnant" and went on to the next card. Evan readily named the shapes as he recognized them, and when I repeatedly asked, "Yes, but how *many?*" I continued to answer my own questions before he could sense any overabundance of eagerness on my part.

My scheme worked out just as I had hoped. Evan could not ignore the challenge of a flash card. He took pride in his proficiency with the cards, and since these new cards were presented as simply a part of that exercise, his desire to excel in this overcame any reluctance he might have had. He almost immediately began to concentrate on calling the numerical quantity of shapes accurately. "One heart—three stars—four squares." I found that he did have some trouble at first differentiating between groups of four and five shapes, but he was so anxious to master the cards that he learned them quite rapidly. Eventually I shuffled the new cards in with the word cards, thus heightening the challenge. He was soon

172

able to identify the number-shape cards as confidently as the word cards. It was a very good exercise for him for several reasons, but the most significant aspect was that, for the first time, he was performing a number feat *proudly*. Pride of accomplishment is, after all, the primary incentive for learning, and now that Evan had experienced this emotion in relation to numbers, the outlook for future number work was promising.

In the area of general knowledge I had decided to broaden my attack on the concept of time. *Time* and *space* were two ideas that were obviously going to present almost overwhelming problems. They are concepts—dimensions really—absolutely basic to man's understanding of life, the world, the universe. Yet, all-pervasive as these dimensions are, they are almost impossible to explain without sophisticated language. I knew that I would have to work with Evan on these concepts for many years. Besides teaching him "sky," "ground," etc., and working on spatial positions, I had done little work with the idea of space. There seemed no way, at the present time, to offer him an awareness of the expanse of country we lived in, other cities, the earth itself. We would wait awhile before starting this. In the area of time, Evan now understood that the words "morning," "afternoon," "evening" and "night" referred to specific parts of the day, and I felt he was ready to go on to learning about "days," "weeks" and "months."

Using a sheet of drawing paper, I devised a unique type of calendar that I felt would best suit my purpose. I also cut a piece of paper into a strip about four by seven inches and placed it vertically in the center of the calendar, securing it with tape on the left side only. This was the "week." I marked off seven spaces with a marking pen and printed the names of the days in these spaces. Using colored pencils, I printed each day in a different color. Tying a bit of red ribbon to a hair clip, I attached

173

the clip to the loose side of the "week" so that it could be slipped up and down with the passage of days. At the upper right-hand corner of the calendar I attached by means of a paper clip a card saying "June." This, of course, could easily be changed. At the bottom right of the paper I taped another small card imprinted with "1969." I was not interested in teaching him dates at this time. I felt they would only have confused him and possibly obscured his understanding of the more elementary idea of the repetition of days of the week.

Every day at the beginning of our lesson, I brought out our calendar, saying, "Here's our week!" Object: to get him to naturally associate the word "week" with the list of days. "What *day* is it, Evan?" I would ask, fingering the movable clip marker. I cannot say that Evan ever really got extremely proficient at calling the proper day, but the important thing was that he began to understand what a day was. More than that, he began to comprehend the meaning of "yesterday," "today" and "tomorrow." "Today is Tuesday, Evan, so yesterday was—*Monday*—and tomorrow will be—*Wednesday*." He also gained an awareness of the passage of months from this calendar and became acquainted with the names of seasons.

"What month is it, Evan?"

"June!"

"And what kind of a month is June?"

"Summer munf!"

Using our calendar daily as we did, Evan became quite comfortable with the concepts involved as well as with the associated word symbols.

Evan had become exceedingly competent and somewhat bored with the puzzles, etc., which we had been playing with during the evening hour. I decided that rather than use this time to extend and reinforce perceptual and academic training, it would be more to his advantage to concentrate on activities that would contrib-

174

ute to the development of the all-around boy. To begin with, we would work at building and perfecting his skill at throwing and catching a ball. This, of course, was a good visuo-motor exercise, but my primary aim was to give him competence in something considered important by all little boys. For months we tossed and bounced balls back and forth across his bedroom, beginning with a large beach ball and advancing to a small rubber baseball. With music in the background—Evan now preferred his sisters' pop records to his own nursery songs —it was a relaxing way to end the day. Some months later Evan was tossing a ball with his father in the front yard when an interested neighborhood boy commented that Evan had "the good arm." I felt our efforts had been fully rewarded.

During Evan's final two weeks at nursery school he began, for the first time in two years, to display negative feelings about going. Our timing in getting Evan into a class at the center was certainly perfect, we thought. He was probably beginning to feel more anxiety over the difference between himself and the other children. Perhaps too, now that they were getting older, the others were becoming more aware of Evan's difference and were beginning to tease him. We could hardly wait to see his reaction to being in a group of children with similar problems.

Evan's class at the center was going to be taught by Sister Martha, who had come out from Indiana just for the school's summer session. Meeting her the week before the class began, Don and I could not help judging her by her appearance. Extremely pretty, with beautifully coiffed white hair, her face exhibited that combination of intelligence and kindness that inspires immediate and complete confidence. This would be a good summer for Evan!

We were not disappointed. Although Evan's class was

not held in the room with the large observation glass, I was able to glean enough to know that the experience was a happy one for him. To begin with, he was eager to go each morning, clambering smilingly into the car. Nor was he ready to leave when I came to bring him home. He would attempt to wave me off with a "Bye, Mama." Also, Sister Martha told me that he was quite cooperative in class and not in the least hyperactive as I had expected him to be. When I, along with two other mothers, accompanied the class on a picnic during the last week of school, I could see that she had not misled me. Although Evan did not play with the other children, he was happy within the group and agreeably accepted indicated rules. Obviously, he felt that he belonged here. Just how much he understood of the other children's problems and his own kinship with them I could not know. Did he really think about his handicap and draw comparisons between himself and others? Or did he just *feel* his problem without mental elucidation? It was something I had often wondered about and would continue to conjecture over, especially when I would see him sitting quietly, absorbed in thought. Expressing his inner thoughts and feelings was a privilege denied Evan, and so he had to form his own conclusions and explanations unaided. It was a very heavy burden for such a little boy.

welcomed fall with enthusiastic anticipation. Just as the past year had been the time of Evan's intellectual awakening, so the coming year must be the season of his social awakening. I was depending on it. Evan would be attending one of the center preschool classes for two hours each morning, and he was to have the teacher I had hoped for. Her name was Gail, and although I had not met her, I had heard enough about her to think she was one of those people with that rare, instinctive "touch." That quality would be a requirement in succeeding with Evan, for he did not respond to conventional approaches. The good summer had strengthened my optimism. Evan had been happy and cooperative in Sister Martha's class, and he had been making gratifying progress in his attitude and performance with his speech therapist. It was now time for him to begin learning to cope with the demands of performing in a group.

At home we had made an arrangement which we were confident would contribute immensely to Evan's social development. Our neighbors next door, the Madsens, had been a part of Evan's small world since his birth. Harry and Irene could hardly have been fonder of Evan had he been their own child. They had suffered with us when Evan's handicap was discovered. Irene was a generous, warmhearted person who was never too busy to help someone out or to pass the time of day with someone who needed a friend. Since Evan had been old enough to play outside, she had made a regular habit of inviting him into her house. There he would sit upon a little stool and "talk" to her as she plied him with cookies. What kind of conversations took place, I can't imagine, but Irene assured me, "We talk. Oh, yes!" The therapeutic value of these social expeditions was inestimable, and the really nice thing about them was that Irene arranged them because she genuinely enjoyed Evan's company. The Madsen's pretty daughter, Linda, had been our baby-sitter since Evan's infancy, thus strengthening his tie to their family. He did not have individual relationships with the two Madsen boys—young Harry, thirteen, and Jimmy, two and one-half years older than Evan—but he was aware of them as part of this almost second family. During the past summer, while Cindy and Wendy were vacationing in Minnesota with my parents, we had seized the opportunity to have Harry do some baby-sitting with Evan. The fact that Evan had almost no exposure to older boys had concerned us for some time. He needed a model, an example, someone to identify with who was not an adult. Unlike a normal little boy, he could not learn how boys were expected to behave from conversation or stories. He needed to be *with* another boy so that he could figure it out for himself. Evan and Harry seemed to be getting on well together. When the girls returned and we could no longer use Harry as a sitter, we looked for another way to continue the big boy-little boy experience. After discussing the matter with his parents, we offered Harry a regular job: spending an hour and a half with Evan every Saturday morning. Harry could do whatever he liked in this time. He did not necessarily have to play with Evan. If he had chores to do or a project of his own, he could proceed as usual so long as Evan tagged along in his wake. The only objective was to allow Evan a chance to be around him. Harry had been agreeable to the idea and Saturday was now becoming an important day for Evan. When I would ask him what he had done during one of these sessions and he would mention "cars" or "ball," I knew that our hopes for his identification with boyish pursuits were on their way to being realized.

So it was with the feeling that we had already started toward the year's goal that I drove Evan to the center on the first day of the regular school term. Leading him to his new classroom, I saw a lovely, dark-haired young woman in the doorway. Probably quite unaware of the fact that she was on her knees, she was intensely absorbed in the effort to make some sort of contact with each child as he entered. This, of course, would be Gail. As Evan tried to slip by unobserved, behind another child, in a typical attempt to avoid a personal encounter, her arms reached out and drew him to her.

"Hello. I'm *Gail*. What's *your* name?"

"Evan," I supplied after a moment when I saw that he did not intend to respond. Gail looked at me for a second or two as if snapping a mental picture of me, then returned her attention to Evan.

"Hi, Evan. I'm Gail. *Gail*." She emphatically gestured toward herself. She studied his face, searching for some clue to the inner child.

"He knows you, Sunny," she remarked to one of the volunteers, sharply noting the glance of recognition with which Evan favored this lady. "Sunny" had helped out in Sister Martha's class and Evan had been especially fond of her. Satisfied that she had observed some definite kind of reaction in Evan, Gail let him go and greeted another child waiting at the door.

As I sped homeward I had difficulty keeping my mind on the road in front of me. I was excited. Gail was all I had hoped she would be, and more. I needed no further proof beyond this brief initial observation. Her intense gaze as she had looked into Evan's eyes, her instinctive little gestures, her emphatic tone were like mine—all forcing him, *compelling* him to focus his mind upon her. I did not need to decode her message, for it was my own: "I *will* reach you. I will not allow you to turn away from me." Surely this person who was so like myself was the one who could lead Evan into that outer world. I wanted to discuss Evan's particular abilities and problems with

179

her, but I decided to wait until she had had a chance to observe him for a while.

During the second week, when I picked Evan up from his therapy session—he still had therapy twice a week, after school—his therapist told me that Gail would like to talk to me when I found it convenient. When Karen had gone over to the classroom to get Evan for therapy, she had found Gail working with him on some colored blocks.

"You know," Gail had said with some excitement, "I think he's beginning to learn his colors!"

"Oh," Karen had laughed, "he knows those." She told Gail of Evan's way of putting people on and of the things I had taught him. Gail had wanted to find out all she could. It was what I had been hoping for; Gail would discover for herself that Evan was not at all what he seemed. How glad I was that this time it was a therapist rather than just "Mama" who could vouch for Evan's carefully guarded ability.

Rising unusually early the next morning, I managed to get to the center twenty minutes ahead of schedule. Gail was pleased that I had complied with her request so promptly. She could not have realized my own gratification at her earnest desire to fully understand Evan. I filled her in on the concepts he knew and the skills he had mastered, and I described the level at which he was currently working at home. I mentioned, as Karen had, that it was his strange habit to feign ignorance about his capabilities. I stressed, however, that his great difficulty in understanding speech was no pretense. His receptive aphasia was extremely severe, more so than most people imagined. Gail listened carefully, occasionally studying Evan, who was wandering about the room. I could see that she was comparing my words with his demeanor, not with skepticism but in an effort to see him as he really was. As the other children began to arrive, I prepared

180

to leave, but first I said a few words to Evan so that Gail could observe my method of communicating with him. To my surprise he tuned me out completely, behaving as if he neither saw nor heard me. The little rascal, I thought. Of course, he would not risk compromising his helpless image in front of his teacher! Gail did not have an easy task ahead of her.

In the following weeks I observed Evan in class almost daily for varying amounts of time. Gail was beginning to get him to verbalize, I noted with satisfaction. Her most effective weapon in fighting Evan's deliberate inattention was sheer perseverance. When he entered the room in the morning, she did not allow him to push past her until he had responded to her greeting with a "Good morning." Getting down on the floor with him, she used much the same tactics I often had in forcing his attention upon me. Taking his face in her hands, she would bend close to him, saying just a trifle loudly, "Evan. *Evan!* Say, *Good morning.*"

After a few attempts to wriggle away from her, Evan would finally compromise with an echolalic, "Say-good-morning."

This would not do. "No, Evan." Gail made a gesture as if wiping a slate clean. "*Good morning.* Good morning, *Gail.*"

Because she managed to convince him that she was quite ready to kneel at the door with him until nightfall, she succeeded in getting from him the desired "Good morning." Soon it was "Good morning, teacher" or "Good morning, Gail," and he was responding to her first, or at least second, greeting. So it went during the entire classroom session. Evan was never just handed crayons, clay, scissors, or juice and crackers. Some effort must first be made to verbalize a response to "Do you want some——?" Insistent though she was, Gail's manner was gentle and affectionate.

Although Evan was making satisfactory progress in speaking in the classroom, I was concerned by the fact that he rarely seemed to perform the activities at hand. If the other children were drawing or working with clay, Evan was sitting with the crayons or clay barely touched before him, staring around at this child or that. What was he thinking, I wondered. His interest in the other children seemed limited to this rather furtive gazing. He never approached any of them, much less attempted to speak to them. When I mentioned my observations to Gail, I found that Evan's lack of performance in assigned activities did not concern her at all.

"I know that he can do those things. I'd really rather have him observing the other children. He needs so much to relate to them."

She was right. As long as Gail realized he was capable of performing the assigned tasks, I need not worry there. His great problem, as she had said, was a total inability to relate to other children. I had known before, of course, that Evan did not make friends. His language disability had set him apart from the children in the neighborhood and at his former nursery school. There simply had been no common ground on which to base relationships. Now that I could regularly observe Evan's behavior in a group, I could see that the problem was not that simple. The other children had language impairment too; some could make no really intelligible sounds at all. Yet these children made overtures toward each other, if not with words then with actions. Evan avoided any personal confrontations. If another child approached him he turned away as if he did not see him.

I knew there was a word for this type of behavior: autistic. I had heard this used in connection with some neurologically handicapped children. The word frightened me. Autism was a severe mental illness, little understood, and anything but hopeful in prognosis. The victims of this tragic disorder live, sometimes exclusively, in a world of their own, apparently unaware of other human beings. Evan was certainly not like the severely autistic children I had read about. Yet in the classroom he was obviously exhibiting what I knew could only be described as autistic *tendencies*. What did that vaguely familiar expression imply, I worried. Was Evan really autistic but to a small degree? Or did it mean that he was not actually within that classification? It was more than a technical question. I had read that true autism was a form of schizophrenia. It was extremely important to ascertain whether Evan was afflicted with that mental illness.

I told Don of my observations and conclusions about Evan's behavior at school. He, too, was disturbed. His knowledge of autism, like my own, was confined to children severely afflicted with the illness. We would have to find out what it meant to have *tendencies* in that direction. Because I found it so terribly hard to ask a question when I was fearful of the answer, it was Don who voiced our apprehensions to Sister Elizabeth.

"Evan," said the Sister, "is what they called autistoid." The suffix -*oid*, meaning like or similar, made a world of difference. Evan was *not* autistic, but certain facets of his behavior were similar to those of an autistic child." We were inexpressibly relieved at having the problem thus defined.

Yet, I thought later, even as Sister Elizabeth had dispelled our greater fears, she had confirmed the fact that Evan had yet another obstacle to overcome beside the ones we knew of. It was easy to understand the cause for his autistic behavior. In his previous experiences with other children, he would naturally have realized that he, alone, was unable to participate in their interchange of communication. Rather than allow them to exclude him, he found it less painful to exclude *them*. Even here at the center, it was possible that Evan did not really understand the fact that the other children also had language problems. Some of them spoke almost normally, and Evan may not have noticed the fact that several had obvious expressive speech disorders. After all, he was accustomed to not comprehending people!

The most significant fact I had noticed about Evan's classmates, which he undoubtedly sensed too, was that they seemed to *understand* speech. During the weeks I had been observing the class, I had eagerly searched the group for other "Evans." They simply were not there, I realized finally. Most of the children had *expressive* aphasia, minimal to severe, or they had more general symptoms of a neurological handicap. I could not seem to find one child with the kind of severe receptive aphasia Evan had. Was it so rare, I wondered? Or—my suspicions began to form—had Evan's receptively aphasic peers, by this age, already been classified as mentally retarded and assigned to accordingly appropriate programs? If I had not begun pouring knowledge into Evan's mind a year ago, would he not now be considered definitely mentally retarded? I was sure of it. I had begun my educational program with Evan in time to avert functional retardation, but at just over three years, he had already acquired emotional complications. Judging from his performance with the first therapist, it was already too late for an outsider to get through to him in time. That wall which surrounded him would only have continued to grow thicker and more impregnable. Who would have guessed the brightness of the child imprisoned within? I shuddered. How many were sealed off in this manner—forever? If only developmental aphasia could be diagnosed at, say, age two; before the child himself begins to reinforce with his own fears the walls of his prison. Yet our own pediatrician had been prepared to wait another four months or so before looking into the reasons for Evan's puzzling slowness. Thank God we had taken action ourselves!

By hard work Evan had won the right to be in the group to which he belonged. But because even here he was different, he stood apart. Somehow, someone had to convince him that he was not alone. Watching him through the observation glass, I was helplessly aware that this was one thing I could not do.

The time had come to say goodbye to Evan's speech therapist, Karen. There was genuine regret on both sides in ending our association, for it had been a rewarding experience for each of us. Karen had been the first professional teacher-figure with whom Evan had sustained an honest relationship. What's more, by reinforcing my own work with him, she had given Evan an inkling of the purpose of my teachings. He now realized that the things he learned from me were things he would be expected to use in outside relationships. As for Karen herself, she said that Evan had made more progress with her than any child she had worked with.

"You really *work* with him!" she exclaimed. "It has just made all the difference. I'm really glad to have had the chance to see the kind of progress that can be made when the mother is conducting her own program at home."

Evan's new and permanent therapist was a young woman named Shana. The only thing that bothered me about Shana was that I had absolutely no idea of what she was thinking. Evan, of course, was trying his new therapist on for size and seeing just how much feigned incompetence he could get away with. I determinedly briefed her with my by now routine pitch concerning Evan's ability-versus-demeanor discrepancy. Shana always listened politely and, I observed, tested him on the abilities I claimed he possessed. When Evan usually declined to reveal his accomplishments, however, Shana made no comment to me at all. She simply continued to listen courteously to what I was beginning to suspect she considered my ravings.

Our lessons at home were proceeding more smoothly than ever. In fact, we seemed to have just passed another milestone. Evan had finally achieved the triumph I had long been seeking in prearithmetic. After he had become readily proficient with the number-concept flash cards, I had made it my primary summer's goal to get him to actually count a number of objects and then tell me the correct quantity. I had once more brought out the blocks, the pins, the pennies—anything I could find for counting exercises. Evan had two distinct methods of inaccurate counting, which he alternated according to whim. Given a row of ten blocks, he might carefully and correctly count them, touching his finger to each as he intoned "one-two-three . . ." up to the tenth block. Then when I said, "Good! *Right.* How many blocks?" he would turn to me with an angelic smile and answer, "Six blocks." Or, given the same row of ten blocks on another day, he would count them *almost* correctly, but this time he would deliberately let his finger slide over one or two blocks so that the last number turned out to be eight or nine. Then to my question "How many?" he would repeat the last named number as he was supposed to. Despite my frustration, I knew he was gaining competence at counting and was probably capable of accurately counting up to twenty-nine objects. As summer had threatened to end, however, with my goal of proper counting unrealized, I had played my last trump—bribery!

Waltzing Evan back and forth along our market's candy counter, I took careful note of the candy that interested him the most. This happened to be a bag of pink and white mints. I did not let him see me buy the candy and instead arranged for it to suddenly appear in my bedroom, temptingly on view in a glass jar. When he spied it and asked for some, I shook my head and led him to the kitchen where I gave him some of the candy we usually kept around. This forestalled the tantrum which would have occurred with a total refusal and still allowed the pink and white mints to remain inviolate. For

188

a week or so I allowed his curiosity and desire to build around the forbidden candy until the glass jar acquired a very special aura.

Then one afternoon I brought out my box of safety pins and lined eight of them in a row for Evan to count. He was using the correct-count-but-incorrect-answer system this afternoon.

"No, uh, uh," I said, thoughtfully shaking my head. Although I always verbalized the fact that his answers were wrong, I avoided behaving as if it were very important. Leaving the room for a moment, I returned with the jar of candy and set it on the table near the pins.

"Do you want some candy?"

"I want some candy!" Evan made an excited grab for the jar.

"First," I said firmly, staying his hand, "count *right*."

Evan counted the pins, this time employing his alternate inaccurate counting method, and again reached for the candy.

"No," I told him. "Count *right*. Do it again."

Evan counted the pins incorrectly once or twice again, all the while nervously eyeing the mints.

"Well, I'm afraid not," I said, reluctantly taking the jar and rising as if to return it to my room.

"Ah—ahhh! I want some candy, please, *Mama!*" Evan protested.

"All right, then." I sat down on the edge of my chair. "Count the pins again, and this time *count right*."

Miraculously, he did it. He actually counted the pins accurately and then declared the correct number.

"Very good, Evan. Very, *very* good," I told him, scooping the pins back into their box with a sweep of my hand. "*Now*, let's open the candy!" It was always important when conquering a mental block to keep too much enthusiasm from creeping into the words of praise.

189

Whether he construed excessive joy in such a situation as triumph, I'm not sure; but it produced a negative effect.

Once we had jumped the psychological counting hurdle, I reduced the counting exercises to two a week. There was no point in overemphasizing something he still had a negative feeling about. At age four and one-half, he would not need to progress further than counting, in the area of arithmetic, for some time. We would take it slowly and casually, and I hoped that Evan would lose his dislike for number skills. There would be so many abstract mathematical concepts for him to wrestle with later on! His present attitude did not made his future in this subject seem promising.

Two or three months later I made worksheets with rows of objects for him to count. This was a progression from counting tangible, three-dimensional objects. Still later, I drew the objects to be counted in formations of two, then three, then four or five rows rather than in one long row. This counting of more than one row of objects was a difficult transition for him. With each new row he would want to start with number one again. With patience, persistence and more bribery, we got over this hurdle as we had the others, until finally I reduced the counting exercises to one a week, just enough to keep his skill polished.

In the area of reading, the flash phrase-cards had served their purpose. Evan had now formed the habit of reading from left to right. It was time to start teaching him to read from a book. The question was—what book? The eighty or so words he was able to read were words I had chosen as the most meaningful and important to *him.* I had not followed any sort of first-grade primer word guide, and there was bound to be quite a difference in my list of words. Also, he was accustomed to reading my large printed words, not publisher's type. It was hard for him to cope with more than one new problem at a time, and just learning to read sentences in rows on a page would be quite enough at the start. Well, there was no other way to go. I'd just have to make his first primer myself.

Looking for a writing tablet that opened from the side, I settled on a bright red eight-by-ten spiral composition book. With a black marking pen and a box of crayons—I had to include illustrations—I went to work. I prepared only a few pages, for I intended to write the book as we went along, according to Evan's skills and needs. I made the words on these first pages two lines (one-inch) high. As his skill and confidence increased with the pages, I would gradually make the words smaller and smaller. The sentences were short and involved meanings Evan could easily understand. The first page went:

> Look, look.
> See the big
> red ball.

My drawing of a red ball over these words covered more than half the page. On the opposite page were the words:

> See the little
> red ball.

My drawing of a ball on that page was a bare inch in diameter. Since the two pages were opposite each other, Evan could readily compare the two drawings and relate the words to the pictures. The next two pages were similar and dealt with the ball being "up" and the ball being "down." After that, my text and illustrations concerned Evan himself—his family, his house, his activities and so forth. The purpose of this was to make it as easy as possible for him to relate to the ideas contained in the sentences and pictures. I made sure that all of the words were *known* words. Reading pages of sentences would be a new enough experience for Evan, without encountering unfamiliar words.

As we began to read the book, I pointed to each word with my pen as Evan was to read it. Later, I pointed only to the first word in each line. He took up the pointing himself with his own little forefinger, which I considered quite all right. After he was accustomed to reading pages, I was soon able to stop my own routine word pointing. I did have to point out occasional skipped words or lines; such skipping is common with NH children. His greatest difficulty in reading the book was in recognizing the first word in each sentence. These capitalized words threw him completely, and he really had to learn such words as if they were brand new. Once I recognized the problem, I began to routinely make his flash cards with the same word on both sides, one with a capital first letter. Thank heaven, we were getting an early start in reading. At least we had time to root out some of these unexpected stumbling blocks. I tried not to worry about the eventual necessary transition to real books.

Evan had finally achieved his first real success in drawing. By demonstration, then guiding his hand, I had taught him to draw a simple face on his blackboard. His independent effort was only a lopsided oval with two small circles for eyes, another for the nose and a scribble for the mouth; but to me it was beautiful. Soon he was adding blobs on each side of the face for ears. I was now teaching him to print his name on the board, guiding his hand through the letters, then letting him make his own attempt.

In the area of general knowledge, our biggest project for the year concerned time. Evan was now quite accustomed to the idea of days, weeks and months, and I planned to spend a great deal of time this year emphasizing and teaching him to anticipate holidays. The first to come would be Halloween. Using pictures of pumpkins, witches, etc., I taught him to identify them early in October. Each day, when I brought out our "calendar" and he had correctly named the month, I would say, "Right! *October.* It's October, so—*what day is coming? Halloween!* Pumpkins, witches—Halloween!" I was directly establishing the proper associations in his thinking.

All of this meant very little to Evan at the time. For one thing, he did not comprehend "is coming." I was sure he remembered past Halloweens, but he did not know now what I was trying to tell him about the occasion; nor probably had he ever even realized that "Halloween" was the name for the night he remembered. I knew, however, that by daily repeating "Halloween is coming" he would understand what I had been trying to convey once that day arrived.

Possibly by Thanksgiving, and certainly with the Christmas season, he would be able to understand what I meant when I said "Thanksgiving (or Christmas) is coming." He remembered several Christmases, if not the name for this day. With visual aids I could refresh his memory on the meaning of that word. Thus, he should be able to understand when the time came to announce that "Christmas is coming."

I would start our holiday anticipations at the beginning of each appropriate month, for I wanted him to connect these days with their months, thus enlarging upon his time concept. To make sure that he made this association, I always began questioning him on the coming holiday as soon as he had named the month on our calendar.

General knowledge was a subject that extended beyond our afternoon lessons. Our morning drive to the center, for instance, was our time for learning about weather.

"What is it, today, Evan? Sun or rain?" To our peril, I was soon able to teach him the meaning of "fog." "Cloudy" was a hard one. When he had learned the different types of weather and understood the question I was asking, I was able to change the question to its more sophisticated form: "What is it today, Evan? What's the weather?" So went our often necessarily backward way of studying vocabulary. He first learned the words for the answers and then the words contained in the questions themselves.

One morning in late October, Gail, his teacher at the center, took me aside for a hurried conference. "I'm not getting through to Evan. I can't put my finger on the cause. I think he probably belongs in the more advanced group but I don't know whether to put him there now or not. I don't know if I'm failing to reach him because he's underchallenged or if it's something else. Would you see if you could come up with anything that might help me?"

Troubled, I told Gail I would do what I could. In my observations I had not noticed any deterioration in Evan's classroom behavior. In fact, the only difference I had noticed since the beginning of the term lay in his increased willingness to respond to her routine conversational gambits. There was by no means a dramatic change so far as these responses were concerned; but whereas before he had refused to verbalize almost completely, he now made reluctant verbal concessions when pressed. What apparently disturbed Gail, then, was not an appearance of any new problems with Evan but the fact that she had not made more progress with him in overcoming the old.

For the next week I concentrated on evolving some new insight into Evan's attitude at school. Carefully observing him in class in the morning, I would spend the rest of the day trying to piece together some understand-

194

ing of the inner feeling underlying his behavior. He liked school and he liked his teacher; I knew that. He was capable of doing most of the things Gail called upon him to do. Yet he would not perform. Why? It was the old problem—feigned ignorance, "putting people on," whatever we wanted to call it. Giving the problem a name, however, did not help Gail with its solution. I, who knew Evan best, must attempt to define for her my own entirely emotional, empathetical understanding of him.

Finally, feeling that I had come as close to finding the words to express my own intuitions as I could, I told Gail I thought I might be able to help her. The following morning after class had begun, Gail joined me in the observation room.

"Well," I began, "I just hope you'll be able to make some sense out of my conclusions. All that I have to give you is a theory. I'm so glad that you have sensed his intelligence despite his performance. His father and I have always thought that Evan is an unusually bright little boy, but the opinion of adoring parents doesn't carry much weight by itself.

"I think, however, that you are overestimating his auditory comprehension. His receptive aphasia is devastatingly severe. I haven't seen any other children here who have anything even approaching it. He has the greatest difficulty understanding even the simplest phrases. What probably throws you is the fact that he speaks better than many of the others. Almost all of his speech, as well as most of the language he comprehends, has been systematically *taught* to him, as if it were a foreign language. He was probably 'picked up' less than ten percent of his language skills. Sometimes you will use words or phrases that, simple as they are, he doesn't know yet because we just haven't gotten to them in our vocabulary study.

"Yesterday, for instance, when you were working with

representations of people on the flannel board, you asked him what the figure of a man was. If you had just asked, 'What's that?' he would have known the answer. We've studied 'people.' But you asked him, 'What does this look like?' He could not have understood you because he has no comprehension of *look like.* It's a verbal concept he hasn't had yet. We haven't studied 'like' and 'different.' I guess it's high time we did, by the way. Many of the questions you ask him I know he *can* comprehend, but he doesn't attempt to respond to these either. This is where the theory comes in.

"I think that Evan is afraid. There is enough language he can't understand taking place to make him feel helplessly inadequate—out of it. With his auditory problem, he may not even realize these children have their own language problems. I think he sees this as a part of that world to which he can never belong. He may feel that if he shows you he *can* comprehend some language, you will begin to expect full understanding from him. He knows he can't possibly achieve that. I know I'm not putting this very well, but I think he'd rather you expected nothing of him than expect too much and find him wanting.

"Perhaps, if you always used the simplest and most basic words and phraseology you could think of, he might be able to understand most of what you say. Then it might begin to dawn on him that he *is* capable of participating here. I know it will be hard for you to know which words to use. It's so easy for me because, as his teacher of speech, I know just exactly what words are in his vocabulary. For instance, he understands 'big' and 'little,' but 'large' and 'small' might as well be Greek. He comprehends, 'Are you finished?' but 'Are you done' or '. . . through' is meaningless to him. The only rule I can give you is to use the most common form of any word or sentence and try another if that does not work."

Gail had been listening closely, occasionally nodding in understanding as she followed my ramblings. "I can see it now. Yes, it all makes sense" she said, slowly. "I've been using the wrong words sometimes. So often I've been sure he knew the answer to something, and yet I felt my question just wasn't getting through. I can understand now, too, how the severity of his problem would make him feel inadequate. I had thought that perhaps he was not participating because he felt the activities were beneath him, but I can see it's probably the other way around. He feels *inferior* rather than *superior.* Still, I think he does belong in the more advanced group, and I would like to transfer him there eventually. But for now, maybe it would be better to keep him here and work on the communication until he feels more secure. The simplest words—I'll keep that in mind. And if I get on the wrong track, be sure and let me know. For that matter, if anything else comes up that you think I should know, don't hesitate to take me aside, at any time."

We watched the children for a few moments. This was their free play period. Gail had found that they settled into their structured activities more readily when they had had this opportunity to unwind. My eyes, as always, traveled to Evan. Although he could easily be singled out as a loner, he was hardly a pathetic figure. Playing among rather than with the other children, he was obviously happy just to be there.

"You know," said Gail quietly, "what you are doing with Evan is going to make that important difference for him. You'll be rewarded a thousand times over—because he's going to make it. You and I have the ideal situation right here: both of us working together and reinforcing each other. We just can't help but win!"

Following our talk Gail began to make slow but definite progress with Evan. With each activity she made a point of giving him individual and carefully simplified

197

instructions and explanations. Soon he began to make some effort toward class participation.

"You were right," she told me. "I can see now how far off I was in estimating the extent of his receptive aphasia. I can tell by the difference in his expression when I speak to him now that before he simply wasn't comprehending me."

I had just resumed my observations of Evan's therapy sessions with Shana after missing them for some three weeks. We had recently finished having a new wing built onto our house and were also involved up to our ears in a speech center fund-raising event, so life had been truly hectic lately. A great change had taken place since my last observation, I saw instantly with excitement. Gone were the elementary blocks, rings and what-have-you, always present until now in these sessions. Shana and Evan were playing tic-tac-toe! He was learning to make *X*'s and *O*'s. He was learning the meaning of *"my* turn" and *"your* turn" and he was becoming familiar with the overall concept involved in playing a game. In other words, he was learning something completely new from someone besides myself! It was another giant step.

I obviously did not have to worry about Shana's appraisal of Evan's ability. She understood him and she certainly knew what she was doing. All that really remained for Evan in accomplishing his intellectual independence was to acquire the ability to learn in a group. I did not expect this to happen overnight, but at least he had now taken all the steps leading up to this last important one. How quickly things were happening!

Christmas 1969 was, in a sense, Evan's first real Christmas. My "holiday-anticipation-plan" in our general knowledge training had worked out just as I had hoped. When I brought out our calendar on the first day of December and introduced the new month to Evan, I started eagerly to work with, "What special day *is coming? Christmas!* Christmas Day is coming!"

I could see that he now understood that I was informing him of a holiday lying in the immediate future. "Christmas tree—Santa Claus—presents—*Christmas Day!"* I prodded his memory with those associated symbols he was most likely to remember the names for.

For the next three weeks we spent at least half of each daily session working at Christmas-related activities. I bought a Santa Claus coloring book and a *Night Before Christmas Sticker Fun* book. Each day I brought these out, and if I did most of the actual work in them, I still accomplished my primary aim of teaching Evan the necessary Christmas vocabulary. I had never realized before how very much of this there was, but Evan rose to the challenge and grew rapidly proficient at identifying "Christmas tree," "Santa Claus," "Christmas wreath," "reindeer," "elf," "present," "candy cane" and on and on. Only a year ago, teaching him such specialized vocabulary would have seemed rather ridiculous, considering the fact that he was only beginning to master such words as "wall," "floor" and "chair." Had it really been only one year?

As we worked at our books, I made a point of occasionally saying excitedly, "*Christmas!* Christmas is coming!" Such repetition, which would have been a great bore to most children, was always necessary in establishing the proper connections in Evan's mind. At the end of our

199

lesson periods I worked at teaching him to sing "Jingle Bells" and "We Wish You a Merry Christmas."

I decked our "halls" early in the season, and this also helped Evan become acclimated to the spirit of expectation. Setting up our little crèche on a corner table, I taught him to identify the principal figures and to recite the fact that "Christmas is Jesus' birthday." I knew that these memorized words meant little or nothing to him and I did not attempt to elaborate on the religious implications of Christmas. This was a time for helping him orient himself in relation to what he could see and hear. Abstract explanations belonged to the future. It was a part of my "familiarization" method to merely implant one tiny seed of an idea for the present.

By the time Evan's class held its Christmas party on the day preceding vacation, he had been thoroughly tutored in the traditions and customs that were a part of the season. Still, I thought, it was all just another lesson to him. He understood what was going on, yes. The Christmas tree, the gold-foil angels, the presents, the carols, the Christmas cookies, the stockings—these were all a part of what we called Christmas. He knew that. But missing was the flush of excitement on his cheeks, the sparkle of anticipation in his eyes. Was all of his childhood to be one long lesson? Could he never know the joys, the special thrills that were normally a part of that time?

Just as the party was almost over, the door opened and Santa Claus suddenly appeared in the room. Evan looked at him, his eyes widening. Then, before any of the others, this child with the *autistic* tendencies made a dash for the bearded figure. All but knocking the jolly old fellow over, he scrambled into his arms.

As I gazed at the incredibly natural picture they made, child embracing Santa Claus, I thought of all the hours of learning, memorizing, reciting, that had led up to this moment. So I was not just "programming" Evan's brain with words and facts, after all. Somehow, unknowingly, I had touched his imagination. Santa Claus had only been a name, a picture on a page, yet Evan had so entirely absorbed the idea of this mythical creature that he could personally relate to him—he loved him! Later, as Evan sat on Santa's lap examining the fluffy white beard, Gail nudged me. "You're really going to have a *good* Christmas this year," she whispered.

We were not disappointed. What had before been only a bewildering mosaic of unrelated events and nameless objects now came into focus for Evan. This was Christmas! Decorating a tree, hanging stockings, opening presents—these were things we did at Christmas. Certain songs, Santa Claus, angels, decorated cookies—these were all a part of Christmas, too. Never again would the word "Christmas" produce a blank in Evan's mind. It was a very special time!

Looking back, I believe that that holiday season marked Evan's transition from baby to little boy. It would no longer be necessary for him to be completely in the dark about what was going on around him or what would be happening tomorrow. The verbal concepts he had indirectly picked up along with the specialized vocabulary words enabled him to cast off the role of the helpless and uninitiated spectator. Just as he had gained confidence from learning the terms we used to refer to elements of our physical surroundings, so he now acquired a measure of security in his own relationship to events. It was apparently enough to enable him to take that first step into the world of "knowing" people. The frustration that had so marked his attitude and behavior diminished perceptibly. He began to conduct himself like a person who was aware of his own adequacy.

In January I began to teach Evan to print numbers and letters as a part of his daily lessons. He was ready for this now, I was sure. He had learned to print his own first name and also to make *X*'s and *O*'s in his tic-tac-toe games with Shana. I decided to begin with numbers. Using both paper and blackboard, I guided his hand through the nine different formations, one at a time, repeating each until he had a feel of the arm motions. I found that this was not the way he wanted to learn. He made no effort at all to concentrate on what we were doing or to try to imitate my motions. However, he did like to study the example numbers I always first printed on his paper. He would attempt to create imitations of them in his own way. He invariably began his formations from the bottom rather than the top, and usually used two separate strokes to make one number. The number *6*, for instance, was a lopsided circle with a vertical line hovering somewhere above it, not necessarily connected. In no other activity had Evan's visuo-motor problems been so graphically in evidence. His was not the proper method to use in learning to print, I knew. But then, he was not like everyone else. He wanted to figure out how to make these symbols in his own way, and I allowed him to do so. As I saw his efforts gradually improve and the floating lines begin to firmly join their proper circles, I became more certain that this was the right method for *him*.

As part of our general knowledge activities, I had already begun a long period of work with the concepts of *alike* and *different*. The easiest way to convey the initial idea, I found, was with shoes. Lining up several pair, I would take two at a time, prompting Evan: "These two shoes are——? Alike!" or "These shoes are . . . different!"

It had been an entire year since Evan had begun to learn to answer questions, but what would have seemed to have been the natural next step—his *asking* them—had never followed. Finding (with some difficulty) certain objects he could not identify, and using my old hint-and-prompt method, I set to work at further programming of his language center. Lifting a ball of cotton into his line of vision and pointing to it, I said, "Evan! Say, What's that?"

"White," said Evan, after thinking a moment.

"No," I said, shaking my head and brushing away his answer with my hand. "Say, What's that? Wh . . . wh . . . what's . . ." I did not accomplish my purpose in one afternoon, nor in two or three. But after several days Evan, for the first time, parroted uncertainly, "What's that?"

"It's cotton. That's *right*, Evan. What's that? It's cotton. That's *right*. Good boy!"

I kept working at the same routine and praising his echo until Evan realized that his part in this exchange was indeed to ask, "What's that?" He had actually learned to ask a question! It was a major breakthrough.

When we had practiced this exchange for several weeks, using quite a succession of strange objects I had hunted up, Evan suddenly realized he could satisfy any of his curiosities with these two simple words. I found myself besieged by a veritable shower of "What's that's?" I had always known that Evan was curious, but now that his curiosity was freed by these two words, I found out the things he was specifically curious about: almost everything. He wanted to know what the egg beater was called, what the furnace was called, what the heel on the loaf of bread was called, and on and on. I was delighted one day to realize that I was actually becoming normally irritated with my child's unending

204

questions. Evan was now in charge of his own vocabulary lessons.

It would be a long time before Evan learned to use any variations on his one question. For now, he seemed to regard "What's that?" as the key to all learning. Strangers were often startled at being confronted by this small boy pointing at them and asking, "What's that? What's that? What's that?" How could they know he just wanted to learn their names?

Gail was going to be leaving the center at the end of this first semester, for she was expecting her first baby in March. Although she was now, to use the biblical term, quite "great with child," she had lost none of the energy and enthusiasm that characterized her teaching. One morning toward the end of January when I picked up Evan after class, Gail approached me with a piece of paper she had been studying.

"I'm going to put Evan into the advanced class," she told me. "We were drawing snowmen this morning and I was trying to get him to make the three basic circles. I didn't think he was getting the idea; he kept making these scribbles instead of circles, and then I looked closer and suddenly realized he was trying to write his name. Look!"

One almost had to know what to look for, but there it was indeed. In less than inch-high letters: *Evan*. He had already learned to print his name at home, but this was always in six-inch-high capital letters. The last three letters in this signature were small case. Gail, as she usually did, had previously printed his name in the upper right-hand corner of his paper, and it was this he had been attempting to imitate. This apparent manifestation of Evan's desire to work at more challenging activities dispelled any lingering doubts Gail might have had in making the decision she had been considering for months.

In the last few weeks Evan had begun to reveal his proficiency at many of the activities the class was working to learn.

"Evan worked three puzzles this morning—just bing! bing! bing!" Gail had told me several days before, shaking her head. Previously he had sat for long periods with this or that puzzle fragment in his hand, behaving for all the world as if he did not know what to do with it.

Gail and I arranged to accomplish Evan's transfer on a Thursday, a little more than a week away. She already had one new child in her advanced group and wanted to get him settled down first. Whereas Evan's present class met from eight-thirty to ten-thirty, the more advanced group was in session from ten-thirty to twelve-thirty. The time change alone would mean an adjustment for both Evan and me. Too, he was more hyperactively inclined during the last half of the morning, and I speculated apprehensively on the effect this might have on his classroom demeanor.

It was probably unfortunate that we settled on Thursday as Evan's first day in the new class, for he had therapy at ten-thirty and was brought to class half an hour late. Obviously wondering over the fact that he had not been brought to his regular eight-thirty class, he expected, nonetheless, to go home with me after therapy, as usual. Surprised, confused, outraged, he was already in a tantrum before he had even reached the door of the classroom. Shana had taken the responsibility of accompanying him to class ("dragging" him would be more accurate). I was already in the observation room, ready to view Evan's first day in his new class. After only a few minutes I wished that I had been a little less than conscientious in my interest. He screamed, he kicked, he threw himself about the room in a way that left me nothing short of aghast. Gail held him and spoke soothingly to him, calmly explaining to the other children—when

206

Evan paused for breath and she could be heard—that since being in the new class was strange to him, he was afraid, and so "we all must try to help him as much as we can." The other children nodded solemnly in quiet understanding and sympathy.

Somehow, Gail and her two volunteers managed to carry on the normal classroom routine, taking turns at attempting to calm Evan. Ignoring the deafening noise that seemed never to end, they put him through the motions of each activity in turn. Pacing distractedly back and forth in the tiny observation room, I was almost swallowing my cigarettes as I lit one after another. This was obviously not going to work out! Gail would tell me at the end of the session that Evan's first day in this class had been his last. I wondered if she realized I was there. Probably not or she would surely come and beg me to please take my child home! I considered knocking on the door and notifying her of my presence. Better not. I didn't want to risk interfering. If only I had gone home! Well, it was too late now. I'd have to see it through to the bitter end.

The class was now having its exercise period. Gail was moving Evan's arms up and down in the appropriate motions and at the same time attempting to keep the still screaming child from collapsing on the floor. "Be careful, Gail," I muttered aloud, nervously conscious of the baby she carried within her.

It was refreshment time and Evan was placed in a chair not twenty inches from the glass I was observing him through. A cup of juice and a cracker were placed on the table before him, and although he appeared not to notice them, his cries began to diminish and at last to cease. Obviously, he had simply worn himself out. I waited apprehensively for him to reenergize himself. He stared, glassy-eyed, at an unseen point as the other children finished their snack. As the day's "helper" began to gather up the empty cups and napkins, Evan, for the first time, began to look around at the other children. Slowly, he reached for his own untouched cup of juice and began to drink it.

"It's been ten whole minutes," I heard one of the volunteers remark to Gail in reference to the comparative silence that had settled over the room. Gail brought out a tape recorder and I gathered from her explanations that the group was about to do something it had never done before. Each child was to speak into the microphone and later hear his own voice played back.

"What's your name?" asked Gail, holding the microphone close to the child on her left. She asked him a few more questions, then moved on to the next child.

"What's your name?"

"Evan. *Evan*." The small voice interrupted the recording attempts of the child whose rightful turn it was. Looking up in surprise, Gail nodded and smiled encouragingly at Evan, who had risen from his seat and approached her. With the tears still drying on his flushed cheeks, he was endeavoring with an odd intensity to make himself heard. He wanted to participate, he was telling her. He wanted to please her. He was seeking, as he never had before, her approval of his effort. Gail had succeeded. Evan was in the group where he belonged and he was accepting it.

Few people could have accomplished what Gail had in placing Evan where he rightfully should have been. Realizing just where his place was, for one thing, required a largely intuitive faith. Even then, she would have failed had she not been a special kind of person to whom Evan found himself relating almost in spite of himself. It was our unbelievable luck that Gail was there at the beginning when we needed her most.

Evan had qualified for the race. Now the real work was to begin. In the ten days before the incoming teacher

208

took up her duties, Evan's behavior was only passably satisfactory. He was, as I had feared, more hyperactive during this later morning session. But Gail seemed confident that he was going to progress here.

The new teacher's name was Gretchen. Blonde and attractive, she had an air of calm efficiency. Since she had previously worked with exceptional children and had children of her own, she had a combination of professional knowledge and personal understanding that well-equipped her for the job.

Changes of any kind require adjustments on the part of all children, but it is particularly hard for neurologically handicapped children to readapt themselves to new situations. For Evan, who was still in the process of adjusting to his new class, the change in teachers seemed for a while to be more than he was going to be able to handle. In a matter of a day or two he underwent what appeared to me to be a complete personality change so far as his classroom demeanor was concerned. Never a classically hyperactive child of the sort who cannot sit still for an instant but must be constantly tearing around grabbing at things, he now affected this behavior during class. It was quite obvious that, for reasons of his own, he was deliberately patterning himself after another child in the class who apparently had been a great problem for some time. The question was whether or not Evan's behavior was symptomatic of a temporary period of adjustment or a new behavior trend.

Phases in our children's lives are only so designated when they are over. As the coward dies a thousand deaths, so the anxious mother suffers a thousand parental failures as she sees her children try out new and attractively unacceptable patterns of behavior. For some four weeks I haunted the observation room, shaking my head and filling up ashtrays. During the third week Gretchen had the number-one problem child removed from the class. Physically aggressive, he upset most of the children, made teaching next to impossible and was obviously not learning anything himself. He was put into a specialized teaching situation for the remainder of the term and from all I could see in his behavior the following fall, this apparently produced dramatically successful results.

With his model gone, Evan began to settle down somewhat. In the fourth week I decided to double his morning medication, and he began to resume his normal behavior. At this time Evan had a new pediatrician who was quite knowledgeable in the use of drugs for NH children. Evan's "normal behavior," however, was puzzling to Gretchen, for his severe *receptive* aphasia and his still somewhat autistic demeanor made him unique in the class.

I'm just not reaching him, Connie," she told me worriedly.

Far from discouraging me, her words were reassuring. They told me she was aware of Evan's problems and concerned about them. If she had said nothing or seemed complacent about his behavior, I would then have worried. As it was, I could only feel optimism, especially since Evan had come out of his terrible phase. (Now I could call it a phase!) I explained to Gretchen as I had to Gail the unusual severity of Evan's auditory problem and gave her what helpful suggestions I could. After a short time Gretchen came up with her own solution to the problem of Evan's lack of comprehension and resulting inattention. Whenever possible, she had a volunteer devote full time to him—repeating instructions, focusing and refocusing his attention, making sure everything got through to him. It was apparent from the beginning that Gretchen's plan was going to work. Evan would make progress here.

Several weeks after she had finished her teaching, Gail

returned to the center to hold individual conferences with each mother. She had carefully assembled each child's work, evaluated it and worked out suggestions and recommendations. I had been looking forward to my own conference with her, for I had something exciting to tell her. Evan had just passed his fifth birthday and we had been apprehensive about the problem of getting him properly placed in school the following fall. Following Sister Elizabeth's recommendation, Evan had been evaluated by the center's consultant psychologist to facilitate his placement. Evan had placed "bright-normal" on the intelligence test.

"And I'm sure that's low, considering his attitude and comprehension problem," said Gail, delighted but, like me, not particularly surprised. It was merely a relief that what we knew to be true was going down on the official record. The greatest fear of parents in facing these tests is that our children might simply be in a noncooperative mood on the designated day. If he placed lower than his actual ability in the tests and the psychologist saw no reason to dispute the score, the child might be mistakenly recommended for a mentally retarded class.

Gail opened Evan's folder and began to go over the contents with me. These included attempted drawings and worksheets of the simplest kind. The worksheets had been specifically compiled for perceptual training and might demand no more than the drawing of a line. The line, perhaps, was to be drawn horizontally in front of an illustration of an airplane to indicate the direction the plane should take, or maybe the line was to be drawn vertically from a cloud to a flower below to symbolize rain. Evan's work seemed adequate but unimpressive. It was really impossible to tell whether or not he understood the ideas involved in the different papers. The little hand forming the wavering lines might have been pushed along by a volunteer. Spending no more than a

211

few minutes on these papers, Gail brought out her own typewritten evaluation of Evan's abilities, handicaps and needs.

"As you and I both know, Evan's greatest problem is his extremely severe receptive aphasia. People who work with him are going to have difficulty realizing this. It's very unusual to see a child who knows so much and still understands so little, auditorily. He has *some* expressive aphasia, but I don't think much, really. His words are clear and he knows his vocabulary. If he can just understand what others are talking about, he can always manage to express what he wants to. What I mean is . . ." Gail paused helplessly, for a moment, trying to think of a more graphic way to describe Evan's problem.

"You mean he knows the answers, he just doesn't understand the questions," I smiled. I, too, had searched for a concise phrase to define Evan's unusual predicament.

"Yes." Gail nodded slowly, considering my description. "Exactly! That's very well put. Yes!" she nodded again, pleased. She resumed: "It's going to be up to you to see that people understand this about Evan. They'll have no way of knowing otherwise. Observe the teachers and aides who work with him, and if they aren't speaking so he can comprehend them, tell them and keep on telling them! Tell them, too, when he is putting them on. All of his progress in school is going to depend upon this. Be sure that they are fully aware of his capabilities. Tell them just as you told me in the beginning.

"Evan's sight reading is really very, very good. I think he's ready for books. You might try him on the Dr. Seuss reading series. There are some very simple books in it, *The Eye Book* and *The Ear Book,* which I'm sure he could read. Also, you might buy a book of worksheets and see if you can get across the idea of doing that type of work. He doesn't seem interested in that sort of thing in class

212

I'll give you the name of a store where you can get some material." She printed an address on the paper before her.

"He needs as much social experience as you can possibly make available to him," she went on. "He needs to learn to relate to people. Just conversation with your own friends is excellent. Give him the maximum exposure to social situations of all kinds. By the way, have you ever thought of teaching him to play cards?"

I blinked. I could honestly say I had not. Evan playing cards? There was a challange!

"There is a lot of social interaction in simple card games, and of course they would increase his numerical skill as well. You might try it." She began to reassemble Evan's work along with her own written suggestions for me to take home.

"Just call me if you run into any problems you think I can help with," she told me earnestly.

It was not goodbye. Gail was going to keep in touch with the little children who were more than pupils to her. Taking my folder, I went to the observation room to wait until class was over. Scanning the little group through the glass, I patted the folder and grinned to myself. Tonight I was going to teach Evan to play cards!

After my conference with Gail, Evan continued to progress both intellectually, as we had come to expect, and also emotionally, as we had only been able to hope. I tried to think only of the fact that he *was* progressing and not to wonder if it was going to be enough. I used many of Gail's suggestions in my own program with Evan. Perhaps the most immediate and significant advancement inspired by our conference lay in the transition to real books in our reading work. I had looked at simple reading books before but found the vocabulary too different from what I had taught Evan and the story ideas too complicated for him. Now I looked again. Because Gail seemed to see Evan exactly as I did, I was inclined to respect her advice above almost any other.

The Dr. Seuss Reading Series is, of course, very well known and has been widely acclaimed for putting some fun into the business of learning to read. Indeed, my daughter Cindy had learned to read from one of his books while still in kindergarten. My chief doubt about using these books with Evan was that, as I remembered, the stories were full of fantastic and whimsically drawn and named creatures. (This was not altogether accurate; I was confusing some of his *story* books with his reading series books.) While delightful amusement for most children, I feared the non-existent creatures would only confuse Evan.

A great number of books had been added to the series since I had last looked at it. I succeeded, without too much difficulty, in selecting Evan's first real "reader." It was not one of the introductory books; I found that Evar had advanced beyond this level. The title of the book was *Put Me in the Zoo*. It was written by Robert Lopshire and concerned an animal somewhat resembling a bear with measles who could do marvelous things with his "spots."

215

Although I knew Evan could probably not grasp the simple plot, I was certain he would be able to relate to the ideas involved on each individual page. The spots changed color, changed size, changed spatial position —in short, all the primary concepts Evan had learned so well were involved in the story. He had also visited the zoo on a number of occasions. There would be no problem relating there.

Once I had gotten the book, I kept it hidden awhile before introducing it to Evan. It contained many words he had not yet learned and I wanted to teach him most of these before he encountered them in the book. For the experiment to prove successful, his first impression should be, "Why, this isn't hard! *I* can read this!" If his first "real" reading experience turned out to be an exercise in frustration, his attempts constantly impeded by strange words, he might decide at the outset that real books were too difficult for him.

Searching through the first pages for words to print on my flash cards, I was suddenly aware of a very stupid mistake I had been making. Since I had first begun to teach Evan to read, I had not been making my small case *a*'s and *g*'s as they appeared in publisher's type. This was bound to cause trouble for Evan! Testing him with words he knew well, I found that the situation was as I had feared. He did not recognize words with conventionally typed *a*'s and *g*'s. Throwing out all of his word cards that contained the offending letters, I made new ones, this time printing the words in the correct form. I drilled him on these words for about two weeks and found, to my relief, that things were not as bad as they had at first seemed. He did have to relearn the words, yes, but it was not as if they were brand new. He was able to make a readjustment somewhere along the way, and as he began to learn two or three of the *g* words for the second time, he began simultaneously to recognize seven or eight others. He accomplished the relearning task in two or three weeks.

When Evan had learned most of the new words appearing on the first ten pages of *Put Me in the Zoo*, I allowed him to begin reading it. The first day's lesson was not overwhelmingly satisfactory as Evan worked to adjust himself to the experience of reading type. On the second day, however, he read through the first five pages with almost no difficulty.

He had made it! He was out of specially prepared materials and into the real thing. He was reading the way any normal child did. So far as this subject was concerned, Evan was performing as a member of that outer world.

In order for him to be able to read "normal" books in a "normal" way, I found that it was desirable, if not necessary, to continue with special teaching methods. I went on with the flash card system but with a difference: Now I had a definite guide to follow in my word selection. I simply chose new words on those pages he had not yet come to. As he progressed in the book I experimented with letting him attempt to learn some words in the conventional way: from merely reading and rereading them on successive pages. I found that he did not learn nearly as rapidly by this method, nor did he retain what he learned as well. I also found that he did confuse words opposite in meaning, as I had suspected he might. He had trouble differentiating between "fat" and "thin," "short" and tall," even though these words looked nothing alike.

I finally settled on a system of teaching which I am still using. I teach Evan half to three-quarters of all new words via the flash card method, choosing of course the most important. The rest I allow him to "pick up." I can only say that the system has proved highly successful.

At an academic supply store I bought a set of flash

217

cards bearing the "ninety-five most common nouns," and over a period of nine or ten months I worked these into our daily vocabulary drills. After a while our stacks of flash cards would become so large that it would not be possible to go through them every day. I would then begin to give him only the thirty or forty most recent words on a daily basis, testing him on the older ones at more and more infrequent intervals. Those few words that he would occasionally forget would go into the Recent Word deck.

Soon after I started Evan in his first real "reader" I began to teach him phonics. Not only did he learn his letter sounds very quickly, he was extremely interested in them. Practically, however, I found that he was only able to use this skill in reading, in ascertaining the sound a strange word began with. Unlike other children, he was handicapped in sounding out the entire word because common sense did not give him a hint as to just what word would naturally fit into a given sentence. Learning to read sentences would be one of the ways Evan would learn to comprehend them.

Following Gail's suggestion I did buy a book of simple worksheets for Evan. My attempts to get him to do this pencil work produced the sort of odd and indirect success which I had not found uncommon in working with him. He would no more do conventional worksheets for me than he would for his teacher. So, discarding the book, I made my own worksheets geared especially for Evan. Since he liked to read, I printed one word at the left side of each paper. If the word were "chair," I would draw three objects on the right-hand side of the page: a bed; below that, a chair; and below that, a table. Evan's job was to either draw a line from the word to the correct illustration or to encircle the correct figure. He did not want to do the work at all, but after much cajoling, and using my last-resort bribery system, he began to perform successfully. Since he continued to dislike the activity, however, I soon dropped it. We now knew he *could* do this type of work and I did not want him to develop a too negative feeling about our home lessons. As soon as I had let him off the hook with the worksheets at home, he began, albeit reluctantly, to do them at school. Why our successes must occasionally take this roundabout route I do not know.

Gradually, Evan's participating in class became more and more of a natural thing. As well as doing his written work, he began to take part in the verbal group activities as a matter of course. I was interested to see that his teacher, Gretchen, used flash cards much as I had employed for quantity-perception training. Her cards were quite large and each had different numbers of red dots. Evan was the very best at either instantly recognizing the correct quantity or accurately counting it if it were a larger group of dots. As Gretchen went around the group giving each child a turn at a card, I noticed that she saved some of the harder ones for Evan. The amazing thing was not that he could do them but that he *did* do them without a trace of reluctance. The same was true of most of the class activities.

"He isn't learning anything new. That is, he's only doing things he has previously learned at home, but he's *doing* them!" Gretchen told me joyfully. We both realized that this was an even more significant step than the final one, *learning* in class, would be. He had cast off his psychological defense, his feigned ignorance. He no longer felt that his presence in the group was a sham, that eventually everyone would realize that he did not belong there. He had discovered that he was a totally adequate member of the group, that his peers were engaged in mastering the same skills he was and that he was fully as capable as they at performing them. My psychological theorizings were actually being realized.

219

Evan's social adjustment had not proceeded so far that he was as yet approaching or reaching out to another child. He still lacked the confidence for such an act. Still, his passive role had become less so. He was openly pleased to *be* approached.

When I realized that Evan was taking his place with his peers, I knew that it was time to force the issue of toilet training. Throwing out all the training pants, plastic pants, etc., I put him in regular pants and allowed him to cope with his problem himself. With his protection gone, Evan was in a dilemma. He had achieved enough social awareness to be loathe to embarrass himself in front of outsiders; nor did he care to make puddles on the carpets. At the same time, he still refused to use the toilet. For a full week he grappled with his problem. His temporary solution was to retain his urine for as long as was physically possible.

For Evan, this was a frighteningly long time. He would awaken in the morning with a flooded bed, put on his pants and remain completely dry until he went outside to play at three-thirty or four in the afternoon, when he allowed the dam to burst. After he came in—and I had him change his own clothes—he again remained dry until he went to sleep at night, whereupon the cycle would begin again. I knew that he must be in unutterable agony most of the time, and I was in a quandary as to what to do. I longed to put training and plastic pants back on him, at certain times, when I had to take him someplace and it had been five or six hours since he had been wet. But I knew that my doing this even once would doom the project to failure, and all his suffering would have been in vain. One Friday, when Evan had been living in this tortuous fashion for a week, we were both supposed to go to the park with his class. Seeing that he was already *in extremis*, I called Gretchen and told her that we would have to be late. I wanted to wait until the inevitable had happened. The morning crawled by—nothing! By afternoon Evan was lying around on the floor, unable to pursue any sort of activity. I decided that today would have to be the day when he made his decision one way or the other. Neither he nor I could live this way any longer. I would not give him his usual "out" by sending him outside to play. We would see the afternoon through together.

By four-thirty I was inwardly frantic. Just how much capacity did a little boy's bladder *have* anyway? Finally I sat him on the toilet and brought him a sixteen-ounce bottle of Pepsi and a glass. Filling the glass to the brim, twice, I easily got him to down the entire bottle in ten minutes or so. Then, with certain little phrases and songs that Evan always thought were terribly funny, I got him giggling. After half an hour of this, Nature would finally be ignored no longer. In spite of himself, Evan paid his first dues to the institution of modern plumbing. His only reaction was surprise.

Later that evening, when he once more began to assume the uneasy expression and stance that are unmistakable in small children, I remarked casually, "Oh, you have to go to the bathroom, don't you?" Inwardly I prayed—please, oh please don't let this remain a one-incident fluke! Evan, however, accepted my suggestion as casually as I had seemed to give it. He was, in effect, trained!

It took him another four or five days to decide that the problem of bowel movements must inevitably be resolved in the same way, but he was capable of making this decision by himself. We did not have the usual after-training period of accidents, nor was bed-wetting a problem. Everything seemed to follow naturally once we had jumped the first enormous hurdle.

The reasons for his tardiness in toilet training were none of the commonly offered ones. His problem was not (obviously) poor control, nor was it a fear of the toilet. It began with his reluctance to relinquish infancy and was compounded by his strong perseveration. To resolve the problem I had to wait until he felt he had a place to go once he gave up his position as a baby. Licking the perseveration factor required, as always, some maneuvering and the employment of any unfair advantage I could muster. There are no guides for a mother to follow in these unusual situations. That is why she *must* be an expert on her own child.

**S**hana had been quietly bringing Evan to his maximum potential in his performance in one-to-one therapy. He had long since dropped all remnants of his false affect with her and now worked with her as openly and willingly as he did with me. Whereas in the beginning Evan had refused to read for her, he now not only revealed his previous knowledge of the subject but was *learning* more new words from her. One of the things she did was to give him written instructions to follow: Close the door, etc. She spent a great part of her time with him engaged in simple conversations, and these probably did more for him than anything else she did.

"I can hardly believe that this is the same little boy I had in the fall," Shana remarked upon one occasion. "You know," she added, "when you used to come in here and tell me that Evan could do this and he could do that, I just thought—Tch, oh boy!" She screwed her features into an incredulous expression.

I laughed, delighted to at last know the truth behind her previously inscrutable manner. Suspicions confirmed! The year had been an unqualified triumph with Evan. Shana, Gretchen and I were all in agreement.

"If he makes as much progress next year as he has this term, he'll be out of the woods," Gretchen told me.

During the summer I concentrated on reading comprehension in our home sessions. This simply meant that as Evan read I asked him questions with each page and called his attention to the fact that the sentences he was reading were illustrated in the pictures. He did not care for being made to concentrate on the meaning of what he read; he just liked words and enjoyed the challenge of learning them. However, if his reading was going to be of any use to him, it would be necessary for him to develop the habit of wresting some meaning from the sentences. This emphasis on comprehension made our reading lessons maddeningly slow and we had time for little else during our afternoon sessions. Actually, though, I felt that this was what summer studies *should* be—a concentration on a special need. Evan had been regularly using his finger to follow the words on a page, and one afternoon I announced, "All right! No finger. Put your hands in your lap. Okay—read!" I found that he had no trouble reading without his finger. When he had broken the habit after a month or so, I had him put his hands back on the book to hold the pages.

Although Evan's reading comprehension improved somewhat during these three months, the greatest benefits of our work appeared later during the fall and winter when we had returned to our usual lesson routine. I found that he had formed the natural habit of studying the illustrations in his books and attempting to relate them to the words. I instituted the practice of periodically reviewing the older books. It greatly increased his confidence to discover how easily he could read these books the second time around. In November, when he began to spend a part of his playtime reading for his own amusement, I felt that our reading program was an unqualified success.

Because our summer lessons were so occupied with our reading endeavor, I devised ways to contribute to the expansion of Evan's general knowledge during the evening play hour. I made a game we called "Holidays," which consisted of a sheet of paper divided into twelve squares, each square consecutively inscribed with the name of a month. I drew and cut out paper Christmas trees, pumpkins, birthday cakes, etc., to fit into these squares. Evan's job was to take each cutout, name it, name the holiday it represented and assign it to the proper month. In a matter of a few short weeks he could name the month almost any holiday belonged to. The game was, of course, only a further extension of my time-orientation program for him.

Since early spring I had been in the practice of making hand-illustrated charts to convey concepts I found impossible to explain. Using twelve- by twenty-four-inch art paper, I had begun with the attempt to teach Evan the idea of *city* as opposed to *country*. On one side of my chart I drew houses, stores, schools, streets and so forth; on the other side I drew bare green meadows, broken only by a few trees and, in one corner, a farm. Evan learned almost immediately to identify "city—town!" and "country!"

Seeing how easily he was able to grasp an idea from even my amateurishly drawn visual images, I turned my artistic endeavors to an even greater challenge: conveying to Evan the concept of the life cycle. I had been concerned for some time over the fact that Evan did not know what the word "grow" meant, and I knew that I must give him some understanding of the word and its implications. Just to give him the idea of something small expanding in size would not be enough. A balloon could do that. No, I must give him some kind of conscious realization that he had been "born," had been a "baby" and would one day be a "man." Did he already understand this? Was it intuitive knowledge? I didn't know. Whether it was or not, it was important to make it possible for us to *verbalize* on the subject.

I began our study by making a chart with ten consecutive illustrations. The first drawing was of a brown dot of a seed. This was followed by the graphic appearance of a tiny green plant which in successive illustrations become larger and larger until in the final drawing it burst into full flower. With this chart I carefully explained the growth process to Evan, using all the applica-

225

ble vocabulary he knew to drive the idea home: "You *plant* a seed in the ground—*put* it in the ground," and "the plant *grows*—gets *bigger*—*grows* bigger."

When we had studied the chart for a couple of weeks, I prepared several small paper cups with a soil mixture and had Evan plant seeds in them. Placing the cups in the kitchen window, I made a point of calling to his attention the subsequent sprouting and growth of the plants. By fortunate coincidence, Evan and his classmates were planting carrot seeds at school at almost the same time, so the new concept received all of its deserved emphasis for him.

Feeling that Evan had truly absorbed the idea of plant growth, and satisfied that he now comprehended the associated vocabulary "grow," "plant," "seed," I turned my energies to the challenge of teaching him about the growth of human beings. This time I made two charts: one following the growth of a boy and one following that of a girl. I made these charts in much the same way as I had the plant chart, and I intended to explain them in the same terms. I wanted Evan to understand that the concept was the same; only the subjects were different.

My first illustration on these charts was a profile of "Mama" showing an X-ray view of a "tiny seed in her tummy." The next picture showed Mama looking much the same except for the fact that the seed had become a small baby. I did not go to the extremes of showing any sort of obstetrical processes. I was merely going to explain to Evan that the baby "comes out of Mama's tummy," tracing the general way this feat was accomplished. The subsequent illustrations showed a small infant gradually growing into a man or a woman. When I explained these charts to Evan over and over again, I followed up the explanation with personal references and explanations: "Evan used to be a baby. Evan *was* a little baby" and "Evan will grow *big*. Evan will be a big

226

*man* like Daddy. What do you want to be when you grow up to be a *man*, Evan? Will Evan be a fireman? Will Evan be a doctor when Evan is a man?" When trying to get across an important concept, I threw proper speech to the winds. The all-important objective was to convey the idea, and if it could be better transmitted with exaggerated baby talk, then that was the tool to employ.

My growth charts had seemed to produce fairly successful results, so I decided to try my hand again at homemade visual aids for our summer evening play hour. It was time to do something about that difficult subject that had been nagging at me for a long time: Evan's knowledge of space or, more specifically, geography. Even the most elementary map was too complicated for a child who did not even know what a map was supposed to represent. Resigned by this time to "making my own," I painstakingly began a map of the United States. The entire object of my effort was to get Evan to see this drawing as a representation of a vast expanse of "ground." My map was dotted with houses and trees rather than names of states and cities. I drew the boundaries of the states but named only four of them; our own and three others he was auditorily familiar with. I had taught Evan certain facts that he could recite by memory-rote but almost certainly did not conceive the meaning of. For instance, he could say that he lived in the "state" of "California," that Grandmother and Grandpa lived in the "state" of "Iowa," that Mr. Nixon lived in "Washington, D.C.," and so forth. Hopefully he would be able to apply these learned facts to his examination and our discussion of this map and achieve some understanding. I drew in the White House, which he knew about, and tried very hard to make the oceans look real. Since he went to the beach quite often, the idea of the ocean along with the trees and houses should help him to perceive my drawing as a "place."

227

When my map was complete I began to bring it out in the evenings and explain it to Evan. We discussed all of the personally meaningful facets of it.

"This is where Mr. Nixon lives. This is the White House. This is where *Evan* lives. This is the *state* of California. This is Los Alamitos. There is *Evan's* house. There is Evan's *school*."

I thought that Evan understood what the map symbolized, but what I felt amounted to the ultimate test of his understanding of both the *map-space* and *calendar-time* concepts soon presented itself. Don and I were planning to go to Las Vegas for a few days. We had engaged an older girl, Judy, who lived in the neighborhood, to look after the children during our absence. For more than two weeks before our departure, I went over both map and calendar with Evan. On the map I pinpointed the "*city* of Las Vegas, in the *state* of Nevada, where Mama and Daddy are *going*" and showed how we would "*go* there in the *car*." I marked both the day we would leave and the day we would return on a new calendar I had made for the occasion, and marked off each day leading up to that time. I discussed the fact that Judy would come and "sleep in Mama's and Daddy's bed" and that Mama and Daddy would be "back" on Sunday.

Evan seemed to be absorbing all of this, but I knew that I would find out if my impressions were correct or not on the morning we left. If he had not truly understood he would be surprised, outraged and fearful at seeing us go.

Such was certainly not the case, however. Evan not only accepted our departure, he had obviously been expecting it. He talked about our going to "Las Vegas— Nevada!" both then and after our trip. The map was *not* simply an image on a twelve- by twenty-four-inch sheet of paper. He understood that it was an abstract symbol. He was now equipped to learn geography!

228

At the end of the summer I took a deep breath and began to prepare Evan for the subject I had been dreading most—arithmetic. If he continued with his negative attitude toward numbers, I could not see how I would ever succeed in teaching him arithmetic concepts. To bolster my confidence, I took a peek into Dr. William Cruickshank's *A Teaching Method for Brain-injured and Hyperactive Children* and boned up on ways of introducing the new subject. Acting upon some of his suggestions, I first taught Evan to recognize "more" and "less" quantities, using groups or stacks of blocks. I then introduced him to adding by using the blocks or my fingers. "One block *and* two blocks is—count them, Evan." When he had become accustomed to this idea of *adding* two quantities together to obtain a total quantity, I gave him problems on paper. These all involved very low numbers at first, the combined sum never being more than five or six. I followed Cruickshank's suggestion of including dots beside each number. Thus, the sum of one and four would have one red dot beside the *1* and four green dots beside the *4*. Below the answer line I would print one red dot and four green dots. All Evan had to do was to count these dots and supply the answer. The whole purpose of this method was to enable Evan to see just exactly what it was he was doing—in other words, to convey the concept of *adding*.

After a few weeks of this I bought an abacus and spent a great many sessions just teaching Evan how to use it. When he had the idea I began to give him simple written sums without the dots, showing him that he was to set up the problems on his abacus and find the answer that way. For about ten weeks he worked with simple addition in this same way, simply getting the *feel* of it. Since this was only his kindergarten year, we could afford to take our time, making sure the basic concept was well established. In November I began to give him numbers up to ten, plus only one. It was then that the final connection of the addition concept clicked into place in his mind. I could see that Evan honestly realized what the subject was all about.

In addition to written sums and abacus, I often gave him his problems orally. "What's six and one? What's four and one?" allowing him to work the problems out in his head. He became very quick and proficient at this. After a month of working with the "plus one's" from every angle, we went on to the "plus two's." Evan learned these very quickly, for the right wheels were now obviously turning in his mind. I began to give him his written problems part of the time without the abacus, and found that he had no trouble doing them. As we progressed to the "plus three's" I began to make it the rule to use the abacus only with those sums he was in the process of learning. Memory-rote, of course, begins to play a part in the learning, when a child is doing the same sums repeatedly, so it is very important to see that he employs the abacus so that he will have to go through the adding *process*.

When Evan had learned his "plus-four's" and "plus-five's," I made flash cards of all of the addition problems he had had and began to give him his addition in this quick way for a while. At the same time, with abacus and paper, we were beginning to work with the concept of subtraction. By using two different techniques I hoped to keep the two concepts separate in his mind. If he were to be doing both addition and subtraction in the same way at the same time, he might easily have confused the concepts themselves.

One day as Evan was zipping through a paper of twenty-four arithmetic problems, I suddenly realized that this was now his favorite subject! He had found a science of absolutes that, once he had absorbed the basic concepts, was not dependent upon language. He was beginning to tell me of new arithmetic problems he was solving all by himself, for the first time.

"Fifty and zero is fifty," he might remark as I was setting the table. Or "Fifteen and one is sixteen." I had never given him these problems; he was not reciting learned material. He was using a *concept* that worked for him on sums he had never even had. He also remarked often during his lesson that, for instance, "Two and nine are eleven," just as "nine and two are eleven," even though he had never been given this sum in the former way. I had thought that I would have to make a point of teaching him that a sum was the same whether right side up or upside down. His intellect, however, had burst the bonds of perseveration in this subject. Arithmetic was fully meaningful to him as few things had been.

Evan was now doing "normal" arithmetic, just as he was engaged in "normal" reading. It's time, I thought. Time for him to be tested again. Was it good enough? Had I done enough? Would he be able to make it educationally?

He had learned to print all of his numbers, letters and even words and sentences. It was barely legible, but for that he had plenty of time. Unquestionably the brain was sending the proper messages to the fingers. That was the really important thing. I still worked at some basic verbal concepts with him in the old way. I was now teaching him "near" and "far." "The red block is *near*, Evan. The blue block is *far*." And we were working on "What is this *made of?*"

And what about Evan's emotional behavior? Had he made enough progress here? I knew that when I saw Dr. Ward I would be discouraged indeed if he had to tell me again that Evan might still grow up to be retarded. Evan must be ready for this test! To round out the "whole

231

boy," we had bought Evan a bicycle with training wheels and helped him learn to ride it. We had also signed him up for swimming lessons and he had learned to swim fairly competently, if not fearlessly. We were still taking him for the swimming lessons in order to build his confidence.

One afternoon as we waited for his swimming teacher, Evan was splashing about in the small wading pool as he usually did before his lesson. Two freckled children, a boy and a girl of about Evan's age, were also in the pool having a delightful time together with several Styrofoam kickboards. Evan remained close to the side of the pool in a typically deliberate effort to avoid getting in their way. He watched the children with interest, however, smiling rather wistfully, shyly. Suddenly his face assumed an intense expression and, looking directly at the children, he said all too softly, "Evan." He was introducing himself! He was taking his first cautiously independent step into that one area of the outer world he had so far not dared to enter—the land of his peers! The two children, splashing noisily, did not hear him. Say it again darling. Please, *please* try again—speak louder!

"*Evan.*" This time the children heard him and glanced at him curiously for a moment but went back to their play. Evan, absorbed in his purpose, had forgotten to include the carefully learned "I'm" in his utterance. The children had probably never heard of the name "Evan" and had not the vaguest idea of what he was trying to convey. Please, oh please—say something to him—*anything!* Why, in God's name, couldn't I have named him Billy or Bobby or Tommy? Who knew when he might dare such a step again if this one was ignored? Please, little girl, little boy, *please!* Suddenly the freckle-faced boy picked up one of the bright blue kickboards and advanced toward Evan.

"Hey, boy! Want a board?"

232

For just an instant the two small boys smiled at each other. Then, as Evan silently accepted the board, the other child went back to his splashing. Evan stood as if transfixed, the blue board clutched tightly in his hands as he gazed happily after the boy. He had been accepted. The boy had treated him as one of his own number. Evan could be a part of this world after all!

Just before Evan passed his sixth birthday, I took him back to see Dr. Ward. It was time for him to tell us what he thought. Evan should normally be entering first grade the following fall. Was he ready? Could he make it? We knew that he would have to be in special aphasic classes for some time, but could he receive his education at his own scholastic age level? These children were usually placed behind their normal peers in school.

Evan's kindergarten year was not going well. He had returned to the center for the term but was now in an entirely different type of program. He and the other children shifted from room to room and from instructor to instructor five times each morning, which made it hard for Evan to personally relate to anyone. Too, there were no observation rooms and, unable to assist in pointing out possible trouble spots, I had sat helplessly by as Evan's teachers failed to bridge the communication gap. Finally Evan had been put into a group where the academic activities were some eighteen months beneath his level—prereading, simple counting, etc.—and he had become more and more withdrawn in class. It was time for Evan to move on. I was sure that Evan was ready for school on a normal age level. Could we find a school that was ready for him?

Don could not accompany us on this trip to the hospital as he was preparing his classes for semester exams. Once more I thumbed restlessly through magazines in the hospital reception room as I waited for Dr. Ward to complete Evan's testing. What was I so nervous about, I asked myself irritably. Evan was undeniably competent. A child who had accomplished what he had would surely have no trouble with a basic intelligence test.

Yes, *I* knew what Evan could do, an unwelcome inner voice answered. But Dr. Ward did not. What if Evan withdrew into himself as he had recently been doing in school and refused to perform the required tasks? Or pretended he *could* not? Well, did it really make any difference what Dr. Ward thought so long as *we* knew what Evan's true ability was? Yes, yes of course it did. There was not only the emotional need for official professional verification of our own beliefs. A practical aspect was involved too. We could not get Evan properly placed in school on the basis of Mama's and Daddy's opinion. The psychologist's conclusions and recommendations were vital.

Suddenly Dr. Ward reappeared with Evan. I glanced at my watch. They had been gone only twenty minutes, a disturbingly short time. The gravity of the psychologist's face did not allay my apprehensions. He would like to wait until another day to tell me his conclusions, he told me. He wanted to consult with someone else about Evan's tests. Perhaps my husband would want to be at our conference too. Walking toward his office with him to set up the appointment, I attempted to glean some hint of the trouble, for his manner left no doubt in my mind that trouble did indeed exist.

"Evan is a very puzzling child," I ventured.

"Yes."

I tried again. "I know he's different. I mean, he's even different from the children in his classes."

"Yes."

He was not about to tell me anything, I could see that. We arranged our interview for the following morning and I hurried home to call Don.

"Evan probably equated the test with a school situation and didn't bother to perform," I told him. "You know how he has been behaving at the center recently. He just won't do even the simple things they give him. He's so bored with it all."

It was a plausible explanation. Nevertheless, Don and I spent the following twenty-four hours in a state of almost unbearable mental agitation. Could Dr. Ward have decided he had made a terrible mistake twenty-two months before when he had assured us that Evan possessed a normal inner potential? Had I made some kind of overachieving freak out of my child? No, no—ridiculous! Perhaps the psychologist had decided Evan was schizophrenic! Did the autistic mask he wore at school signify a serious mental illness after all? There were no satisfactory answers. We must simply wait.

"It's no surprise. We expected it. We knew there would be emotional problems," Dr. Ward said the next morning.

"Is it serious? He's not—schizophrenic." I asked the question that had disturbed me most since our last meeting.

"No. Autistic behavior is the best dodge in the world for a child with this type of handicap, but he's not really schizophrenic."

"Anyway, Dr. Ward," said Don, "Evan usually only behaves this way at school. He's anything but autistically inclined at home. He was beginning to really adjust at school last year but this year he's been grossly under-challenged and we believe he's feeling bored and—well—put down. He's supremely competent intellectually. His reading is approaching a second-grade level."

Dr. Ward raised a skeptical eyebrow. "He could be just memorizing what he hears, you know," he put in tactfully.

"Oh, no," I shook my head vehemently. "I've taught him with flash cards. I'm sure he must have scored fairly high in the intelligence test, didn't he?"

"No. No, he didn't," the psychologist answered. "I'm sure now that Evan has a normal potential *inside*. I

237

couldn't even tell you that when you first brought him to me. Still, though, the way his intelligence comes *through* is below normal."

"But he does read *so* well and he can print and he's even doing basic arithmetic. He's ahead of himself in these areas," I argued, puzzled.

Dr. Ward looked at me thoughtfully, the raised eyebrow again betraying his skepticism. "I'd like to see Evan again," he said suddenly.

"Would you like him to bring some of his books and read for you?" Don asked him.

"Yes, he could do that, but I'd like to use some of my own reading material too," replied Dr. Ward.

I was instantly both excited and apprehensive. The psychologist was going to test Evan's reading! What if Evan pretended he couldn't do it? Better to leave Dr. Ward in doubt over Evan's reading ability (as he obviously was) than to have it on record that Evan had failed.

Our appointment was for the following Tuesday and on Monday I kept Evan home from school, ostensibly because he had a slight sniffle. Actually, I hoped the day at home would put him in a more cooperative mood for the reevaluation—perhaps erase that "school" association Evan apparently had with the testing procedure. He just *must* show Dr. Ward what he could do! Evan's future in school hung on the psychologist's recommendation.

When Evan and I met Dr. Ward at the hospital on Tuesday morning, Evan rose eagerly from the hobbyhorse on which he had been seated and exclaimed, smiling, "Dr. Ward!" He took the psychologist's hand and went with him in a more than willing manner. Well, that was encouraging anyway, I thought. Eyeing my watch, I became more and more optimistic as the minutes ticked away. This test was taking longer than last week's. That was a good indication that Evan was per-

238

forming more extensively. Thirty minutes—thirty-five—forty—good! They were coming back!

I jumped to my feet. "Did he cooperate? How did it go?"

The psychologist beamed. "Wonderful!" he exclaimed. "He did everything gladly and willingly—his reasoning is on a good six-year-old level and I think that this ability can be developed to a superior level. It will give him something to compensate with while his language skills are developing." He paused and looked at Evan who was wandering about, inquisitively examining the room. "Well," he exclaimed in a positive tone, "he certainly *can* read!"

Evan had done it! He'd done it! I could hardly contain myself.

"You know," Dr. Ward smilingly confessed, "I just really could not believe you the other day. That he could read. You knew it, too."

I nodded, laughing. I had also mentioned to him that my claims for Evan were usually met with disbelief. I showed him some of Evan's arithmetic papers which I had brought along.

"That's good, very good," he remarked, examining them with interest. The eyebrow remained firmly in place today.

"You know, Dr. Ward," I confided before leaving, "we think Evan is going to make it."

"Oh, I *know* he will," the psychologist replied with complete assurance. "We'll do something about his school situation, too. I'll send the necessary letters and so forth and see that he is properly placed."

As Evan and I left the hospital, I saw that the sun had come out, dispelling the earlier gloom of the day. "I *know* he will," the psychologist had said. He was not a man to toss out casual remarks that he did not mean. He had never given us any false hopes, anything he could not factually justify. His remark was as good as a promise. The words that for so long had been confined to our own hearts were now being voiced by the very person whose task it had been to teach us to live with doubt. Squinting in the bright sunlight, I looked at Evan as I took his hand, and silently, with new certainty, I repeated the words to myself: *"I know he will!"*

# *Epilogue*

Evan is currently enrolled in the public aphasia program in our neighborhood school district. This program is in a regular school with normal classes, and the program's goal is integration. There are seven aphasia classes, six to eight children to a classroom, and a teacher and an aide for each class.

When he was first enrolled in the program, Evan was put in the lowest class, chiefly because his language skills were below those of the other children. Last fall he was advanced two or three levels. He is now in a class with children some eighteen months older than he. What he lacks in language he compensates for in other ways. His teacher told me, for instance, that he is far and away the best reader in the class. He is working at the normal academic level.

Our homework sessions still go on. I work on a variety of subjects such as history, for which I type and illustrate Evan's texts. Our chief worry these days? That of many parents of eight-year-olds: That he will turn up in the next county on his bicycle. Competent and self-sufficient, he has been discovered on the curb of busy boulevards, impatiently pressing the traffic button until the light turns green.

Nervous, I am. But I, who first urged him to try his wings, will not tie them back now.

241